From Jerusalem to Antioch

The Gospel Across Cultures

Jerome Crowe, C.P.

A Liturgical Press Book

THE LITURGICAL PRESS
Collegeville, Minnesota

Cover design by David Manahan, O.S.B. Mosaic detail, Antakya Museum, Turkey, 4th century. Photo courtesy of Hugh Witzmann, O.S.B.

1 2 3 4 5 6 7 8

Library of Congress Cataloging-in-Publication Data

Crowe, Jerome.

From Jerusalem to Antioch : the Gospel across cultures / Jerome Crowe.

p. cm.

Includes bibliographical references.

ISBN 0-8146-2432-4

1. Jerusalem in the Bible. 2. Bible. N.T. Acts–Criticism, interpretation, etc. 3. Bible. N.T. Epistles of Paul–Criticism, interpretation, etc. 4. Jerusalem–Church history. 5. Antioch (Turkey)–Church history. 6. Christianity and culture–Middle East. 7. Church history–Primitive and early church, ca. 30–600. 8. Missions–Middle East. 9. Missions–History–Early church, ca. 30–600. I. Title.

BS2545.J4C76 1997

270.1–dc21 96-51702

CIP

For my brothers,
especially Noel, Des, and Brian

Contents

Preface

Brothers of mine, Australian and American Passionist missionaries in countries like Papua New Guinea, Korea, and Japan, speak of the kind of conversion they underwent during years spent outside their homeland. They talk of having set out "to carry Christ" to another world, and of their gradual discovery of the risen Lord already present in one or another of his many disguises in the new world to which they were sent. Some have been content with the task of "planting and watering," leaving the harvesting to another generation. Many of them have lived long enough to marvel at the way the seed they carried from their homeland has bloomed in wonderful new varieties in that different soil and climate.

What happens when the gospel is carried from one world to another and a Christian community is born in a new culture? How does the dynamism of the gospel reshape the culture in which that mustard seed is planted? How does that culture in its turn enrich the Church with new ways of self-expression and a deeper grasp of its own identity?

We should be able to find answers to our questions by studying what happened when the gospel was carried from the homeland and culture of Jesus to the new world of pagan Hellenism. This book is a case study of that first example of the transculturation of the gospel, of the way in which the good news of Our Lord Jesus Christ, so firmly rooted in Jewish soil, was successfully transplanted into a very different culture. The experience of the missioners of our time parallels that of the people who carried the gospel from Jerusalem to Antioch.

Modern research has thrown a great deal of light onto each of those worlds and given us a better understanding of the origins of the Church in the culture of Palestinian Judaism and the ways in which it adapted to the new world. These pages attempt to distill the results of technical studies in a simple form for the reader who wants to get an overview of the way the same gospel was expressed in very different ways in those two cultures without the distraction of footnotes or quotations. For those who wish to peruse particular topics more deeply some added reading is listed at the end of each section.

Many people influenced the development of this book, not least the many generations of students who have shared the journey from Jerusalem to Antioch with me and attended so lightheartedly to the education of their teacher. To the faculty of Yarra Theological Union in Melbourne I am indebted for a decade of friendship and generous collaboration, especially to its president, Fr. Tony Kelly, C.Ss.R., and its registrar, Mrs. Kathleen Moynihan. To the foresight and open-mindedness of my colleagues in the Religion Studies Department of the University of South Australia and in particular to Professor Norman Habel I owe the opportunity to teach in the first Catholic Studies section in an Australian university. Michael O'Donoghue has been a consistently cheerful presence and encouraging leader. I owe a special debt of thanks to Margaret O'Toole, from whom I relearned so much theology, for her constant stimulus and support.

Experience of the Church in Papua New Guinea cannot but force insight into many aspects of mission. Apart from regular fraternal hospitality from Papua New Guinean Passionists I must acknowledge the warm hospitality of the staff and students of Holy Spirit Seminary in Port Moresby, the national Catholic seminary, a unique example of cross-cultural communication of the gospel, where students from every part of that nation and a bewildering variety of its eight hundred language groups are taught by lecturers from Europe, Asia, India, America, and Australia. Papua New Guinean students who communicate with one another across local language barriers in pidgin, their second language, are taught in their third language, English, spoken in an astonishing range of accents. Daily life is a regular transformation of Babel into Pentecost. Never was seminary more aptly named.

Jerome Crowe, C.P.
October 18, 1995
Feast of St. Luke

Introduction: A Tale of Two Cities

In Antioch the disciples were for the first time called "Christians" (Acts 11:26).

Within a decade of the death of Jesus in Jerusalem a completely new kind of community bearing his name came into existence in Antioch. The gospel first proclaimed in Palestine by Jesus in the towns and villages of Galilee and then by his disciples in Judea and Samaria had been transplanted from its mother earth into foreign soil. It had taken root in the capital city of a province of the Roman Empire three hundred miles away.

Jerusalem

Jerusalem was the heart of the Jewish world. In the thousand years since King David had captured it and made it his capital Jerusalem had come to symbolize the whole history of the Jewish people and its vocation as chosen people of the only true God. Though many more Jews lived outside Palestine than in Palestine itself the Temple in Jerusalem remained for Jews everywhere the focus of Jewish worship. It was the monumental sign of God's presence among the chosen people and the center of pilgrimage for Jews from far and near. It was the center, too, of Israel's hopes for the future, for in God's good time, it was hoped, all the nations would join them in their pilgrimage to Jerusalem to pay homage to Israel's God.

Jesus had joined his people on pilgrimage to Jerusalem. He had taught in the Temple. In Jerusalem he had died, and there he rose from the dead. Here was born the first community of his disciples. They had been convinced by the testimony of the eyewitnesses and had come to share their belief that Jesus was no longer dead but alive with a new life and a new power.

That first group of believers had no reason to think of themselves as anything but a Jewish community. They were all Jews, most of them from Palestine and speaking the same Aramaic tongue as Jesus. They obeyed the same laws as he had. They listened to the same Hebrew Scriptures, prayed the same prayers as he had learned as a boy, sang the same folk songs. They celebrated the same feasts and shared in the same worship as he did in the Temple.

Antioch

Antioch belonged to an altogether different world. It had been founded in 300 B.C.E. by Seleucus I as capital of the dynasty that bore his name, the Seleucids. Seleucus named it after his father, Antiochus, one of the generals of Alexander the Great. Antioch typified the Hellenistic culture that was the bequest of Alexander and his successors in the East. It abounded in temples to its different gods. Its characteristic monuments were its many temples, theaters, gymnasiums, and the architecture of a Hellenistic city.

By the time of which we write, Antioch also typified the awesome power of the Roman Empire, which controlled most of the known world. A century before, in 64 B.C.E., the Romans had displaced the Seleucids and made Antioch the administrative and military center of the important province of Syria. It had grown to prominence as the third greatest city in the Roman Empire.

Not long after 35 C.E. people began to notice a new kind of community in Antioch. Greek-speaking Jews driven out of Jerusalem by religious persecution had carried the message about Jesus to the Jewish synagogues of Antioch. Then with breathtaking initiative they had proclaimed their message to non-Jews as well, and these Gentiles, too, accepted their message. By this unimaginable leap they bridged the immense gulf between synagogue and marketplace, between Jews and pagans.

So was born a community that included both Jews and Gentiles in an unheard-of fellowship. Everybody in Antioch knew who Jews were, their separateness, their strange religious usages, their special diet, even the quarter of the city they lived in. Everybody in Antioch, too, was familiar with the welter of religions that other people practiced. What was unknown to anybody until then was the kind of religion in which non-Jews shared with Jews in a way that seemed to transcend previous differences, where Jews would accept the hospitality of pagans, where pagans and Jews could share in common worship, even in a common meal.

Hence the name "Christians," coined, it seems, by pagans and probably by Roman administrators. The term came from the simple creed, almost a password, which summarized the common belief of this new group, "Jesus is the Christ." The Greek word *Christos* meant "anointed one"; it was the Greek translation of the Hebrew word we know as "Messiah." The term "Christ," which the new group used as a title to express their faith in Jesus as Messiah, was mistakenly assumed by others to be his proper name. The followers of Jesus became known as "Christians" or followers of Christ.

From Jerusalem to Antioch

Jesus had proclaimed the gospel in his native Aramaic, drawing his illustrations mainly from the village and rural life of Galilee. Even if the earliest Jerusalem community prided itself as more cosmopolitan than their country cousins from Galilee, their faith still found expression in the same language, the same customs based on family and clan, the same worship centered on synagogue and Temple.

In Antioch, however, both Jews and pagans spoke Greek. Here the gospel was proclaimed in Greek by missioners who had never been in Galilee and had not even known Jesus, to people whose lives were spent in the urban environment of a Roman metropolis. In this transition from the Jewish to the Hellenistic world they confronted situations entirely different from those encountered by Jesus in Galilee and never envisaged by his first followers in Jerusalem. Yet despite the formidable challenges they met in gaining a foothold in the new world, they discovered quite soon that it offered unsuspected opportunities for the spread of the gospel. Before long it was plain that the gospel was as much at home in Antioch as in Jerusalem.

This book follows that journey across cultures, the journey from Jerusalem to Antioch. What impact did the gospel born in the world of Jesus and Jerusalem have on the Hellenistic city? How did the dynamism of the gospel give new shape to the way of life of Christian communities? And conversely, what impact did the Hellenistic culture of Antioch have on the gospel? How did the gospel shed its Jewish garb and take on the clothing of its Hellenistic hosts? How was the Church enriched by this interaction between gospel and culture with a new understanding of its own identity and mission?

We shall look for answers to these questions in a detailed comparison of the two communities, the groups of Jewish believers in Jerusalem and the groups that made up the Christian community of Antioch. We shall examine how they came into existence and the kinds of people who joined them, the way they preached the gospel, the patterns of their prayer and worship, the work of their teachers and prophets, the structures of their community life. In these diverse ways the one gospel of Our Lord Jesus Christ came to expression in different worlds.

Sources

Our basic sources of information on these two communities are the Acts of the Apostles and the letters of Paul. The Acts is the only sustained narrative that deals with this period of history. Paul knew the first groups in Jerusalem personally and shared the life and work of the Antioch community. Modern research has its own special contribution to make. Literary studies, historical discoveries, and the work of the social scientists help to throw light on the religious groups in existence in that world and thus to provide a framework inside which to place the communities we are studying. The methods developed by feminist scholars in particular have drawn attention to the position of women in the life of Jesus and the ministries of women in the early Christian communities that was previously neglected by male scholarship.

The Acts of the Apostles

The Acts of the Apostles provides us with a story that, at first sight, appears as a straightforward and quite detailed account of the first community in Jerusalem, its early missionary activity, and the steps leading to the founding of the Church of Antioch. Its first five chapters are devoted to the events that brought the Jerusalem community into existence, the commissioning of the apostles by the risen Lord, their transformation at Pentecost, the first proclamation of the good news, and the earliest encounters with the hostility of Jewish leaders. A series of cameos presents the first community, the apostles, the community's heroes and villains, all in characteristic poses, gathered in prayer, preaching and sharing their possessions with one another.

Then Luke introduces the figure of Stephen, whose martyrdom triggers a persecution that forces the good news north and south through the ministry of Philip in Samaria and Gaza. There follows an interlude on the conversion of Saul, which takes him from Jerusalem to Damascus, back to Jerusalem, and thence to Tarsus. We follow the spread of the gospel along the Palestinian coast by the ministry of Peter, which culminates in the admission of the first of the Gentiles to the community. The outreach of the gospel comes to a climax in the founding of the Church of Antioch by missioners from Cyprus and Cyrene.

The picture is one of steady growth unimpeded even by persecution, which simply provokes the spread of the gospel by scattering missioners far and wide from Jerusalem. Harmony reigns; friction between different groups is promptly resolved. The mother community in Jerusalem simply acknowledges the surprising work of the Spirit in the mission to Samaritans and Gentiles.

When we draw on Luke to establish the historical picture, however, we need first of all to appreciate the kind of book he is writing. He is not like a modern television commentator, forced to analyze the significance of events as they are happening. He is writing fifty years after these events. He looks back over the first half-century of Christian history and assesses the contribution of key figures, the significant initiatives, the great turning points in the action of the Spirit leading from the beginnings in Jerusalem to the Church he knows in the eighties.

Every history is selective. Luke omits items we would like to know. There was already a Christian community in Damascus when Paul was led there, blinded on his journey, but we hear nothing of how it started. Nor do we hear anything of the beginnings of the community established in Rome well before his arrival there. Luke concentrates on the cities; we hear nothing of mission in the rural areas, of communities in Galilee, for example.

Luke tells the story of the first decade as a series of shocks administered by the Spirit to the Jerusalem community. Scandalized by the attacks of Stephen on the Temple, they are stunned by the surprising success of the mission of Philip in Samaria. Then Peter is obliged to recognize the action of the same Spirit in the household of a pagan, the centurion Cornelius. The climax comes with the reception of the good news by the pagans in Antioch.

We cannot be sure that this is precisely the order in which the events took place and how much of the sequence is due to Luke's dramatic arrangement. There are sufficient clues in his story to show that his picture of harmony and unison existing in the Jerusalem community and spreading through the various churches as the pagans are incorporated into the community by a final official decision in Jerusalem is a stylized presentation.

He does not mask the signs of discord and diversity, the human realities of conflict, criticism, and disagreement.

Luke's story, then, will have to be used critically to help us build up a picture of the communities in Jerusalem and Antioch and the journey between them. It is clear that he has reliable information about both places and may have lived in both and even traveled with Paul, but the details of his story will have to be sifted carefully to establish an accurate historical picture.

Letters of Paul

When we come to Paul, however, we are dealing with somebody who knew the Jerusalem community at first hand, both as persecutor and as member, and who later lived and worked in Antioch before commencing his missionary career with a group from the Antioch Church. His letters were written in the decade between 50 and 60, only twenty to thirty years after the resurrection and the beginnings of the Christian movement. Though he regularly insisted on his own claim to the title of apostle, he talks of other apostles before him, lists the established witnesses to the resurrection, acknowledges the position of the Twelve, and talks about his meetings with the authority figures of the Jerusalem community. This kind of eyewitness testimony is invaluable in itself and helps us to assess the historical value of Luke's story.

What is quite as important, though, is the way in which the letters of Paul permit us to reconstruct so much of the life and teaching of the Church before him. The earliest of those letters was written within ten years of his stay in Antioch. His letters offer us samples not only of the way he used to preach in the forties and fifties but even of the catechism in which he was instructed in the thirties at the time of his admission to the community. When Paul writes "I handed on to you what was also handed on to me," then we are in touch with the tradition of the Church of Antioch and even that of Jerusalem within a few years of the death of Jesus.

The epistles that Paul wrote in the fifties are veritable gold mines from which we can extract nuggets of early Christian tradition, which show us how the earliest believers thought, for example, about the death and resurrection of Jesus, and how Christians before him understood the Lord's Supper. We can find acclamations and prayers from the earliest worship of the Jerusalem community. It is even possible in his letters to detect extracts from the work of early Christian poets and songwriters attempting to put words to their feeling for God and the Jesus they experienced as a living presence in their midst.

Paul's writings are our earliest example of the encounter of the gospel with Hellenistic culture, its new problems, and new opportunities. We see there the work of Paul and other Christian teachers spelling out the moral demands of the gospel in circumstances entirely different from those of Jesus. We can see them developing patterns of Christian moral instruction, incorporating the best of the moral wisdom of the pagan philosophers and teachers into the age-old teaching of the Jewish Scriptures and the Christian insight enshrined in the teaching and example of Jesus.

In Paul's letters, too, we catch a glimpse of the community's various ministers at work, its apostles, teachers, prophets, leaders, evangelists, healers, administrators. We join those communities in their worship and see the way the gifts of the Spirit served to build up the body of Christ.

Modern Research

Modern research has contributed to our picture of those early Christian communities in several ways. Literary techniques have helped to separate earlier from later layers of Christian tradition. Historical discoveries have added a wealth of detail to the picture of the Judaism from which Christianity was born. The methods of the social sciences have brought new insight into the economic, social, and cultural situation of groups within the early Church, and feminist scholars have developed new approaches to the reading of ancient texts.

The main literary techniques concerned, those of form criticism and redaction criticism, were developed between 1920 and 1960. Redaction criticism studies the final literary product, the Gospel of Luke, for example, and separates the contribution of Luke, his own literary and editorial activity, from the materials he drew on. Form criticism studies these materials, individual pieces like sayings or stories, and attempts to establish the function they served in the life of the community and possibly the circles in which they originated. To these may be added the discipline of source criticism, pioneered much earlier in the nineteenth century, which seeks to establish the extent of written sources an author employed.

It has become clear that the gospel stories about Jesus were shaped in oral transmission in view of community needs. Preachers used them as illustrations of their message, they were recited in worship, and used in defense of Christian belief against attack by other Jews and in justification of community practices. The sayings of Jesus were adapted to provide answers to new questions and situations. We come to see Christian prophets and teachers at work adapting the message of Jesus to changing circumstances. Careful literary and theological analysis of the so-called Q source, the material shared by Matthew and Luke but not found in Mark, has reminded us of the diversity among the earliest groups of Jewish believers in Jesus outside as well as inside Jerusalem.

The major historical discoveries of recent times have been those of the materials discovered at Qumran on the northwestern shores of the Dead Sea from 1947 to 1954. The Dead Sea scrolls give a very detailed picture of one particular Jewish religious group, or sect, which has some close similarities with the community in Jerusalem as Luke describes it. Together with other documents of this era these show how wide, at that time, was the range of Jewish thought and belief, the variety of "Judaisms," as they have been called, and the spectrum inside which the new Jewish group must be placed.

Since the 1970s the methods of the social sciences have been brought to bear on the history of early Christianity. Scholars have drawn on the findings of sociology, social history, and anthropology to explore the relatively neglected area of the social situation of Jesus and his disciples and that of the early

Christian. They have studied the impact of social, economic, and political factors on the origin and growth of the Jesus movement. Models developed in the study of more modern societies have been applied to the worlds portrayed in the New Testament texts.

This kind of research has shown the importance of an understanding of typical social attitudes and behavior in Roman-occupied Palestine and in urban centers in the Roman Empire. It has provided new insight into the social dynamisms involved in the development of Christianity, from one of many competing Jewish renewal movements to an independent and influential religious movement, and the ways in which Christians made sense of life in their changing world.

Feminist scholars have contributed in two main ways. They have shared and given direction to historical research into the position of women in the Jewish and Hellenistic worlds, their education, and their participation in public affairs. More significantly, they have developed approaches to the interpretation of those ancient texts that make allowances for the influence of the patriarchal world in which they were born and in which they have been interpreted for centuries. This has helped to reconstruct the world behind those texts and recover the obscured or forgotten features of the women companions of Jesus and the women who shared in the ministry of the first Christian communities.

Part 1

Jerusalem

1 Jerusalem

The City of David

A thousand years before Jesus was born King David captured Jerusalem and made it his capital. Strategically situated at the southern end of a ridge of the central mountain range of Palestine on the fringe of the Judean desert, rugged terrain and steep slopes made it a natural stronghold known as "Fortress Zion." David had commenced his career as a guerilla fighter in the south, then been accepted as king by the southern tribes of Judah and later by the northern tribes as king of Israel. When his troops stormed and captured this fortress it was renamed "the city of David" (2 Sam 5:7, 9) because it belonged to the territory of neither the northern nor the southern tribes. It was the royal city, center of a united kingdom of Israel and Judah.

At that time this "city" was not much more than fifteen acres in extent with a population of perhaps two thousand inhabitants. What began as David's political and administrative center became the religious center of all the tribes when the ark of the covenant, the symbol of Yahweh's presence and of the covenant to which all the tribes subscribed, was introduced into the city of David in solemn procession. The ark became the symbol of God's protection for both the city of David and the Davidic dynasty.

In the time of David's son Solomon (961–922 B.C.E.) Jerusalem doubled in area and population as the administrative apparatus increased and building programs flourished in his effort to make it a cosmopolitan, international city. It was Solomon who built the first Temple on a hill a little to the north, in which the ark was installed with great ceremony as its permanent home. Solomon's Temple thus became a national shrine for all the tribes as well as a royal chapel for the Davidic king.

After the death of Solomon the unity of the twelve tribes was shattered by rebellion and schism. The northern tribes of Israel had their own king established eventually in the city of Samaria, while in the south the successor of David continued to rule over Judah from Jerusalem. Though northern kings tried to assure the loyalty of their people by building competing sanctuaries on their borders at Dan and Bethel, the Temple in Jerusalem continued to command the allegiance of people in the north for the four centuries of its existence.

In the centuries that followed, the Temple in Jerusalem stood as massive visual evidence of Yahweh's protective presence. A splendid worship developed with its special rituals, feasts, processions, and sacrifices and its different functionaries, priests, Levites, choirs, and assistants. Its center was the Holy of Holies, or most holy place, the inner sanctum entered only by the high priest once a year, the place of the mysterious presence of Yahweh, the mighty king, enthroned on the ark of the covenant.

The name Zion came to designate not only the mountain on which the Temple was built but the whole Temple complex as well. Jerusalem was "the city of the great king"; Zion was the holy mountain, the dwelling place chosen by Yahweh. The intensity of feeling that the Temple inspired in the faithful Israelite is expressed very clearly in the group of psalms known as "songs of Zion" (Pss 46; 48; 76; 84; 87; 122; 125). On arrival in the Temple the pilgrim was invited to gaze on its walls and towers, so many symbols of God's protective power. The Temple appears as the creative center from which God's power reaches out to assure the fertility of the land and the protection of the chosen people.

The growth of the city continued when the northern kingdom was overrun by the Assyrian army in 721 B.C.E. and many

Israelites fled to the south, swelling its population to as many as twenty-five thousand. Reforming kings like Hezekiah (716–687 B.C.E.) and Josiah (640–609 B.C.E.) heightened the importance of Jerusalem and the Temple by their efforts to abolish the many smaller local shrines, which fostered the worship of foreign gods, and tried to focus the worship of their people more sharply on the sacrificial worship of the Temple.

In the catastrophe of 587 the Babylonians destroyed Jerusalem, reduced Solomon's Temple to ruins, and put an end to the Davidic dynasty. In the fifty years of exile in Babylon that followed, the chosen people, shorn of all they held most dear, were obliged to rediscover their identity as people of Yahweh. Far away from the Promised Land, bereft of Temple and Davidic king, they were obliged to find new forms of worship, new patterns of leadership, new ways of expressing their identity as "a people set apart."

When Babylon's empire was overcome in turn by the Persians and Cyrus freed the exiles to return to Jerusalem in 538 with the surviving treasures of Solomon's Temple, what they returned to was a ruined sanctuary in a defenseless city in a territory reduced to the status of a small district of a province of the worldwide Persian Empire. Under the urging of the prophets Haggai and Zechariah, the faithful Jews who returned from exile in Babylon in 538 finally rebuilt a much more modest Temple, which was dedicated in 515. Since the Davidic monarchy no longer existed, leadership passed into the hands of the high priest and the new class of scribes, the scholars and interpreters of the Law of Moses, which, by concession of their Persian overlords, had become the law of this insignificant territory of Judah.

The City of God

By the time the Second Temple was built Jerusalem had long since ceased to be the city of David. Never again would the Temple be seen as the royal chapel or the sign of God's protection of the Davidic monarch because no descendant of David would ever occupy the throne. Once any kind of identification of the city with Israel's human king had clearly been eliminated, however, Jerusalem itself stood out so much the more clearly as the city of Israel's God and the Temple as the preferred dwelling place of Yahweh in the center of the chosen people.

The one true God, they believed, had chosen this place as the divine abode. They knew that no temple, however magnificent, could contain God's immensity (1 Kgs 8:27-30), and they had learned in the destruction of 587 that no human building could ever provide an automatic assurance of Yahweh's protection for a faithless people. During the Exile the prophet Ezekiel had seen the divine glory departing Jerusalem to take up residence among the exiles themselves. The lesson of the Exile was that Israel's God was most clearly present not in human constructions but in the life of a people obedient to God's will. Zion, the name of God's dwelling place, could not be confined to a hill nor even to a temple; it must apply to the whole people. With the completion of the Second Temple Yahweh would take possession of this building, which would become God's special dwelling place among the chosen people. God's real throne, however, could no longer be the ark of the covenant, long since destroyed, or indeed any material replacement, but the hearts of a people lifted to their God in praise.

The Incursions of Hellenism

The people that emerged from exile in Babylon with a purified faith and newly organized way of life, to reestablish itself in a reduced and impoverished land, was to undergo a more intense and lasting test in the Hellenistic era, the three centuries between the conquests of Alexander the Great, who captured Jerusalem in 332, and the coming of the Romans in 64 B.C.E. When he died in 323 Alexander's empire was divided among his generals. After a century under the control of the Ptolemies from Egypt, Palestine was annexed by the Seleucids in 200 and governed from Antioch, their capital in Syria.

Alexander and his successors brought with them the Hellenistic culture of the Greek city-states. Convinced of their racial and cultural superiority, they exported their way of life into their subject countries. Wherever Greek soldiers settled down after their military service Greek cities sprang up. The Greek language and the way of life of the ruling class were readily imitated by members of subject peoples. The Greek approach to leisure and to the body, its emphasis on sports and athletic contests, were a natural drawing card to the young.

Neither Ptolemies nor Seleucids forced the Jews to adopt the Greek way of life but permitted them to live by their ancestral laws. There were many Jews, however, particularly among the upper classes and the Temple priests, who could not resist the attraction of these modern and exciting Greek ways; though to others this seemed like a simple capitulation to a new kind of cultural and religious imperialism. The Jewish high priest Jason, who had bought his position in 174 from Antiochus IV, favored the new Hellenistic culture and tried to transform Jerusalem into a Hellenistic city. He built a Greek gymnasium, which was placed under the patronage of pagan gods and became a social center in competition with the Temple.

Much worse was to follow. Antiochus desecrated the Temple by robbing its treasury. He quartered his troops in the city, then launched a savage persecution against observers of the Jewish Law. The Maccabees responded by a successful revolt, which lasted for over thirty years and eventually restored both religious liberty and political independence. By 142 B.C.E. Simon Maccabee was recognized by the Seleucid king as high priest, governor, and commander and accepted as such by the Jews. By the turn of the century the successors of the Maccabees, known as the Hasmoneans, were styling themselves "king." Jerusalem was once again, however briefly, the capital of a Jewish kingdom, the center of its religious, political, and economic life.

Herod the Great

The national sovereignty won by the Maccabees was lost in a power struggle between two Hasmonean princes, each seeking the support of the victorious Roman general, Pompey, who had put an end to Seleucid rule. From 63 B.C.E. Judea was subject to the Roman province of Syria. The last fifty years before the birth of Jesus were dominated by the rise and reign of Herod the Great, who was to rule Judea as a vassal king of the Roman Empire from 37 to 3 B.C.E.

Herod was a ruler of great energy, assiduous in flattering his Roman patrons, ruthless and indeed paranoid in stamping out any possible opposition, even from his own family. He engaged in vast building programs, which founded new seaports like Caesarea, cities like Tiberias, and fortresses on the scale of Masada. Jerusalem became more and more a Hellenistic city, with its theater for drama and musical performances, amphitheater for gladiatorial and athletic contests, and hippodrome for chariot and horse races. For himself Herod constructed a magnificent palace in Jerusalem as well as renewing the fortress and barracks that overlooked the Temple. Jerusalem enjoyed the kind of economic prosperity that further separated the rich and aristocratic classes in their magnificent, lavishly decorated homes from the very poor, who were crowded into cramped accommodation in another quarter of the city.

Perhaps his greatest undertaking was the rebuilding of the Temple. Though little remains today of Herod's Temple, recent excavations have confirmed that it was one of the marvels of the ancient world. Work commenced in 20 B.C.E. and was still in progress well after the death of Jesus. First the surrounding valleys were filled to construct a platform 500 yards long and 350 yards wide, an area twice as large as the Roman forum built by Trajan. The massive retaining walls incorporated gigantic blocks up to 40 feet long and weighing as much as 20 to 100 tons. One of those blocks recently unearthed by archaeologists weighs over 400 tons. When eventually the existing Temple was demolished and rebuilt, its exterior was adorned with gold. "No one has seen a truly beautiful building" ran a Jewish saying "who has not seen the Temple of Herod."

The Time of Jesus

In 6 C.E. Jerusalem was made a Roman province governed by a Roman prefect. One of the sons of Herod the Great, Archelaus, had succeeded his father as ruler of Jerusalem and Judea but was deposed by the Romans after complaints about his brutality. The administrative and military center of this Roman province was situated on the coast at Caesarea, though a garrison of Roman troops was installed in the fortress adjoining the Temple, and this was reinforced at the time of the great feasts. Since Rome regularly used the local aristocracy in the administration of subject provinces, the Jewish Sanhedrin, composed of the high priest, aristocratic priestly families, scribes, and elders was the main governing body. Pontius Pilate commenced his term as prefect of Judea in 26 C.E. It was to last for ten years before he returned to Rome in disgrace.

By the time of Jesus Jerusalem was once again a major city with a cosmopolitan culture and an urban center surrounded by a cluster of villages and towns. During the Roman era Jerusalem doubled in size, until it covered an area of 450 acres. It is much more difficult to establish the precise population, though it may well have been 80,000 or more out of a total Palestinian figure of 2.5 to 3 million. At pilgrimage times this figure was probably more than doubled, since the Temple made Jerusalem the major center of pilgrimage in the world.

The Temple remained the heart of the city. Jerusalem was poorly situated as a trade center, since it was not located on any important trade routes and relied on the Temple for its financial support. Jews at home and abroad paid an annual tax to support the Temple. Together with the revenues it produced, especially at the time of the great feasts in the period from March to September, this provided for the upkeep of the thousands of Temple attendants, priests and Levites. It was also the source of the great wealth of the aristocratic priestly leaders who controlled it. At the same time there were many people living in Jerusalem who were directly dependent on charity.

Great Jewish teachers like Shammai, Hillel, and Gamaliel made the city a center of Jewish learning that attracted scholars from as far away as Babylon and Egypt. Paul was to boast that he had sat at the feet of the great Pharisee scholar Gamaliel as one of his disciples (Acts 22:3). There were schools, too, where a Jew could master the kind of Greek learning and rhetoric that we can observe in the letters of Paul, which was necessary to preach and explain the Law to middle- and upper-class Greek-speaking Jews.

Then as now Jerusalem was home to a great variety of Jews. The majority were born in Jerusalem or Palestine, but there were many migrant Jews from all parts of the world who returned to make their home or to spend their latter years in the shadow of the Temple and in the place where they expected the resurrection of the dead would take place. The great majority of these migrants spoke Greek, some of them never learning Aramaic. It has been calculated that some 10 to 15 percent of the population of Jerusalem spoke Greek as their mother tongue, while many others spoke Greek fluently. There were a number of Greek-speaking synagogues in Jerusalem where they could worship and study the Torah in their own language.

This variety extended beyond language to other aspects of Jewish life. As we shall see later, Judaism at the time was a kaleidoscope of groups distinguished by political views and religious beliefs, political and religious radicals, members of baptist movements such as the one led by John, and apocalyptic enthusiasts. There were Pharisees and Sadducees, and an Essene community, too, is mentioned in documents of the time. Recently archaeologists claim to have discovered a city gate known as the Essene Gate in the southwest section of the city, close to sites traditionally accepted as centers of the early Jesus movement.

One might think from a reading of the Synoptic Gospels that Jesus made only one visit to Jerusalem at the climax of his career, but the Fourth Gospel makes it clear that Jesus had friends there and that he joined his people in their journeys for the pilgrimage feasts of Passover (John 5:1; 13:1) and Tabernacles (John 7:1-13) and for the celebration of Hanukkah (John 10:22). He is engaged in healing, teaching, and controversy. No passage of the Gospels talks of Jesus offering sacrifice in the Temple, though it seems natural to assume that he shared in this way in the worship of his people.

There can be no doubt about Jesus' respect for the holiness of the Temple. The episode of the cleansing of the Temple (Mark 11:15-17) shows his indignation at its profanation. At the same time, the Gospels record an enigmatic saying (Mark 14:58; John 2:19) in which he points to its transitoriness and final replacement. This message is spelled out with detailed clarity in the discourse on the fate of Jerusalem and the Temple (e.g., Mark 13:2).

Other gospel sayings show Jesus as a prophet aware of the part Jerusalem is to play in his death. The history of Jerusalem has shown that it has first claim on the blood of its prophets (Luke 13:33). For all his efforts to offer God's maternal care, the Holy City has become the focus for the opposition and hatred that will bring about his death (Matt 23:37-39).

2 The Friday and Its Sequel

Beginnings

It had been a slow learning process. It was only when they began to recover from the first violent emotions–the shock, the grief, the fear, the anger, and the flight of the Friday, that the men and women who had followed Jesus to Jerusalem realized how far Jesus had led them from their Galilean beginnings.

In the beginning they had been attracted to him as a charismatic leader, somebody cast in the same mold as John the Baptist, though different. A holy man, a prophet like the prophets of old. A healer, an exorcist, a teacher . . . but something more. That mysterious "more" was difficult to grasp. Once, after they had been with him for some time and in a moment of enthusiasm, Peter called him "Messiah," as if he were the heir to all King David's glory, the leader God would give to restore Israel to its golden age of greatness. Jesus had refused that title and had referred to himself in a paradoxical way as "Son of Man," teaching them a lesson about the part suffering and even death were to play in his vocation.

The Message

He spoke little of himself. What he talked about was God and the coming of God's own reign. He proclaimed the imminent arrival of a new and final era, of all his people ever dreamed and hoped for through centuries of oppression. The time when the one and only God, the God of their fathers, of

Abraham, Isaac, and Jacob, would assert himself publicly and undeniably as ruler of all, Jews and pagans alike. When that hour struck goodness would be acknowledged, suffering and respect for God's Law rewarded, and evil, oppression, sickness, and death would be brought to an end . . . forever.

John the Baptist, they knew, had spoken in similar vein. What was different in the message of Jesus was his claim that the new and final age was already present. God was indeed exercising divine mastery over the world, and this was happening in the life of Jesus. Not only in deeds of power, when he healed the sick and cast out devils, but equally in the forgiveness and reconciliation he offered to sinners and people usually written off as irreligious and beyond the pale.

The Change of Attitudes

Because God was already knocking at the door in this way, Jesus called for a radical change of heart in order to accept God's offer. The basis of this change was an attitude to Jesus himself. Unless you accepted his message as that of God's herald and instrument of the new age, no other change was possible. Once you accepted this claim, however, then the process of repentance, or change of heart, began to invade all your attitudes and judgments and change your whole life.

This is what had happened to the disciples, men and women, who had followed him in his final journey from Galilee to Jerusalem. When they looked back they could see the changes that had happened gradually to them as they assimilated something of his attitudes through their daily association with him. He had invited them to share his own attitude to God. He summarized it in the term *Abba,* as if his address to God could find no better term than the one he had used to Joseph as a child and grown man in Nazareth. There was indeed something special about his own relationship to the Father, something that could only be learned from him. They learned his understanding of what it was to be God's Son in his absolute obedience to God's word and his trust in his Father's care.

From him they had learned, too, a new approach to religion. A true child of his people, Jesus looked to the Scriptures as the word of God. But he understood the Scriptures in a way different from that of other Jewish teachers, and he read lessons in them that other teachers had not found. He even went beyond the words of the Scriptures to reformulate for the new age the will of God they had expressed for earlier times. In those words, too, he found light for the personal choices he had to make.

They were struck by his freedom. Other devout Jews sought to serve God by very exact study and observance of the Law of Moses. Jesus did not share their meticulous approach to its details nor their veneration for the traditions that had grown up around it. He was unconcerned by the touch of a woman reduced to isolation by its prescriptions concerning ritual defilement, and he was willing to converse with women in public. Even in his attitude to the splendors of the Temple and the holiness of its worship there was something other than uncritical admiration. There was certainly an angry rejection of the abuses that profaned it but also a kind of detachment, a refusal to accept this sign of God's presence among the chosen people as a necessary part of the new age that was dawning.

In his company there was an unusual kind of equality between men and women disciples. Unlike other Jewish teachers he accepted that women had a right to religious training and discipleship. From him the disciples had learned the lessons of the primacy of love over law and the need to offer forgiveness even to one's enemies. They had learned that to accept the gospel he proclaimed was to enter into a world that capsized one's previous values and committed one to learning and living a set of beatitudes at total variance with those of this world.

He had commissioned twelve of them as leaders. They were counterparts to the first fathers of the twelve tribes of Israel, leaders but also symbols of a renewed Israel that had finally achieved the vocation for which God had created it. They had all come a long way since leaving possessions, careers, and families to join him in his itinerant way of life. For all their slowness to learn and his rebukes for their dullness, their ambition, and their lack of trust in God, they had shared in his joy in the discovery of that other world, the kingdom he proclaimed and into which they had entered. They had shared in his mission, his message, and healing power.

The Friday

What happened on the Friday came as the supreme temptation to their faith. It called into question everything they had come to regard as the bedrock of their lives, and it laid bare their own inconstancy and capacity for betrayal.

It was all over so quickly. When one of their own number turned informer, it had been the simplest exercise of police power to arrest him in the midst of his fearful followers, who offered no resistance. An easily arranged legal process had led to the inevitable fate of anybody who could be portrayed as the slightest possible threat to the power of the Roman occupying authority. Within twenty-four hours Jesus was dead. He became one more criminal whose name joined those of the thousands submitted to the ultimate degradation of crucifixion.

These dreadful events stood in such flagrant contradiction to all they had come to believe. In those hours his charisma had deserted him as completely as his disciples. None of the power that had healed others could help him avoid his own fate. The unrelieved ignominy of his death seemed to label him as one cursed by God. It signaled the total victory of his enemies and seemed to discredit him finally as a spokesman for God.

The Aftermath

Worse still, for his disciples it seemed to discredit the kingdom and the God Jesus proclaimed. He had claimed the new age was dawning in his life and work. But he was no longer with them, and the power structures of the old world were even more firmly entrenched. If God was such a Father as Jesus proclaimed, how could he treat in this way the Son in whom he delighted? How could one trust as Jesus did in a God who stood idly by while earthly power and armament oppressed and killed the innocent?

The death of Jesus, finally, seemed to make a nonsense of their experience of discipleship. It left them looking like deluded fools, the laughingstock of their villages, for putting their trust in Jesus and trying to live life his way. They had sacrificed all that men and women hold dear to follow a deluded leader in search of an illusion.

As for the future . . . well, where else could they go but back home? Their leader once put to death there was nothing to hold them together. Not his message of the coming of God's kingdom, which seemed to die with him. Not his commission to lead a renewed people; Israel remained unchanged. They, the supposed leaders, had been revealed as nothing more than cowardly fair-weather supporters.

Not all of them, however. The women had followed him to Calvary, seen him die, prepared his body for the burial, and followed him even to the tomb. Nor could any of them, men or women, however frightened and bewildered, deny the reality of what they had experienced in his company. He had led them into another world, and they had tasted its powers. The aftertaste lingered.

On the Third Day

The recitation of the Creed has accustomed Christians to the phrase "on the third day he rose again in accordance with the Scriptures." Taking this phrase together with the details of the gospel stories that place the discovery of the empty tomb and the first appearances of the risen Jesus on Sunday morning, it is easy to gain the impression that the near despair of the disciples on the Friday was changed to lasting joy within a period of forty-eight hours.

Closer examination of the gospel stories shows that for some of the disciples–those, at least, who fled Jerusalem to return to Galilee–that period may have been considerably longer.

It is notoriously difficult to establish the succession of events related in those stories, since each of the evangelists tells the story in characteristic ways and with contradictory details of time, place, and person. The traditional phrase Paul uses, "on the third day according to the Scriptures," is itself a stereotyped way of underlining the action of God in a significant event. It is intended to describe this act of God as the climax of a series of such acts in the course of the history of the chosen people. It is a theological statement rather than a chronological detail.

The Great Reversal

The Jesus movement, it seemed, had been dissolved by the irreparable catastrophe of that Friday. His death had shown Jesus up as one more messianic pretender. The hopes of his followers had been buried with his remains in the finality of the tomb.

The sequel was to reverse, and more than reverse, that Friday situation. Quite soon the disciples were proclaiming that what followed was without parallel in all the dealings of God with his people. It could only be the final, definitive act in the long history of salvation. In a way as mysterious as it was decisive God brought the demoralized disciples to the conviction that Jesus, crucified so recently in Jerusalem, now lived and acted as a dynamic presence among them wherever they were.

It happened to the women first of all (Matt 28:8-10). The gospel stories single out Mary Magdalene as the first witness to the risen Jesus and underline her role as "apostle to the apostles," the woman who proclaimed the good news of the resurrection to the incredulous male disciples (John 20:18). It happened to individual men like Peter (Luke 24:34) and to groups of close disciples, like the two travelers on the road to Emmaus (Luke 24:13-35). It happened to the eleven, to other groups, even as many as five hundred together (1 Cor 15:5-8). It happened at different times and places, in and around Jerusalem, on a journey, in daily occupations like fishing on the lake in Galilee. How long these happenings continued is uncertain.

The apostle Paul could claim that he had the identical experience as many as five or six years later on the road to Damascus, and we have no indication of when Jesus appeared to James, one of the relatives of Jesus who did not understand or follow him during his life.

The Gospel Stories

The familiar gospel stories of the appearances of the risen Jesus are very different from modern news reports filed by reporters on the spot. Those initial encounters, the manner of perception of his presence, and the ways by which he brought the disciples to faith were far too mysterious to be captured in a photographic record that could then be used as tangible proof to believers and nonbelievers alike. Those stories are the end result of continued attempts over a period of fifty or sixty years to spell out the significance of the happenings that lay at the origin of the Christian community.

Their details convey the understanding acquired in those decades of reflection. Scenarios, individual responses of participants, dialogue–all these owe a great deal to the skills of successive generations of storytellers and teachers who employed the narrative devices they found most useful in communicating the gospel message. Each evangelist tells the story of the eyewitnesses in such a way as to speak to the experience of the risen Jesus by Christians of a later time and a different place.

Different though they are in details, the stories insist on two elements in particular. They emphasize that the initiative in these happenings lay with God or Jesus, and they insist that what the eyewitnesses encountered was none other than the Jesus they had known. Crucified, dead, and buried, he was now present very much alive among them, though in a new, different, and mysterious form.

Those to whom it happened described their experience as a revelation by God. God "revealed his Son," "made him to be seen" (Gal 1:16); Jesus "appeared" to them (Luke 24:34). The best way they could explain this experience was as a kind of "seeing," a recognition, an "in-sight" into Jesus present to them in a new way. This was something quite different from ordinary eyesight. It was compatible with elements of doubt and fear (Matt 28:17). It could be gradual; one could actually be in that presence without realizing it (Luke 24:16). If they had finally overcome their doubt and hesitation it was because the risen Jesus whom they encountered himself acted to open their eyes.

The effects of these happenings were a joy and peace that put an end to their sense of loss, their grief and anger. There was a sense of forgiveness, of release from the guilt of their flight and denial. Scattered groups of disciples found a new cohesion and sense of purpose, an irrepressible energy in bearing witness to what they had seen and heard.

Some of these effects were immediate and may explain what brought them together again in Jerusalem for the feast of Pentecost within two months of their return to Galilee. Other effects were more gradual. Over the years and decades as they pondered the foundation of their community they came to understand more clearly the implications of that founding event.

The Implications

If Jesus had been restored to life then God had established before all the world the innocence of Jesus and the righteousness of all he stood for. The resurrection authenticated Jesus as God's spokesman and stamped God's seal on his message and way of life. All Jesus had proclaimed about the kingdom of God was guaranteed by this divine act. The new age Jesus proclaimed was actually upon them in this spectacular triumph of God over evil and death. What Jesus had promised on God's behalf was being offered to God's people here and now.

God had shown himself as the *Abba* of Jesus indeed. Jesus had shown himself as Son of God during his life in his trust and his abandonment to what he judged to be his Father's call, even though it led to abandonment and death. His claim had been vindicated. Now God had declared Jesus Son by endowing him with divine power. They had sought to understand his mystery by defining him as Messiah; now they saw that it is the risen Jesus who defines the mystery of the Messiah.

Their own discipleship, too, was marvelously confirmed. They had not wasted years of their life in a gamble on a lost cause. In fact, in following Jesus and sharing his life they had been taking their first steps in the kingdom. Far from being taken in by a false prophet, they had put their trust in somebody whose mystery they had hardly grasped but which had now been revealed as far exceeding even their wildest hopes.

As for leadership, they had learned in a bitter school the reality of temptation, the possibility of infidelity and even denial. But his continuing presence among them was both his assurance of forgiveness for their infidelity and a reminder that their commission as leaders came not from their own human leadership potential but from his enabling power.

There were other more troublesome implications. If Jesus had been vindicated so triumphantly as God's spokesman, then how could he possibly have been condemned by the highest and holiest court in the land? How had it happened that their leaders and teachers, all those who seemed best qualified to recognize Jesus as God's envoy, had condemned him for blasphemy? To proclaim Jesus as risen and hence the God-given Messiah would be to expose his trial as a travesty of justice and to invite certain opposition and even persecution from the people responsible for his death.

Mystery and Symbol

The first believers described what had happened to them with the aid of a number of images. The image that was probably the earliest and has certainly become by far the most popular over the centuries is that of the resurrection. "God raised Jesus from the dead," they proclaimed, or "You put him to death; God raised him to life" (Acts 2:23-24).

The image of rising from the dead comes from a particular kind of Jewish writing known as apocalyptic literature, which is exemplified in the book of Daniel. Writing in a time of terrible persecution, the writer envisions the situation of the many Jewish martyrs who seem to be cut off forever from God by the very death that was the most heroic expression of their fidelity. God's justice could not permit such a separation; those faithful followers would be raised from the sleep of death to take their place in "the world to come," which would replace this present world so flawed by oppression and evil.

There were other images in which they tried to communicate what had happened. They found another favorite image in the Psalms that described God's "exaltation" of the Messiah in the ritual act of enthronement of the king. They pictured Jesus enthroned, "seated at the right hand" of God, acclaimed as "Son of God," the triumphant king who exercised God's own power on God's behalf. Convinced that this climactic event was the act by which God had fulfilled all the promises ever made to the chosen people, they could express the mystery in terms of any of the promises for the future that the Scriptures recorded.

Over the centuries the term "resurrection" has passed into common currency as the tried and trusted symbol, or code-word, a one-word crystallization of the mysterious event that lies at the origin of the Christian faith. Time often debases a currency, however, and for many modern Christians "the resurrection" simply signifies something that happened to Jesus. This is to devalue the Easter mystery by reducing it to the individual triumph of Jesus and to ignore what lies at the heart of the mystery, the element on which the Creed insists in the phrase "for us and for our salvation." The resurrection is the act by which God established a new solidarity between Jesus and the human race, a relationship that enables him to remain a continuing presence, offering God's power for salvation to those whose humanity he continues to share.

3 One More Jewish Sect?

The Spectrum of Sects

At first the "Jesus movement" looked like one more Jewish sect. Certainly they had no reason to think of themselves as anything but Jews, nor, for that matter, did anybody else. Jesus had been born and raised a Jew. His message had been addressed in thoroughly Jewish language, style, and imagery. He saw his mission as addressed to the house of Israel. His message was a final call to rise to the level of its vocation as people of the God of its fathers.

His disciples, too, were all Jews. They shared the faith and hopes of their people, their expectations, and their misconceptions. In Jesus, dead and risen, they found the fulfillment of those hopes. They saw their mission as witnessing to the arrival of the new age inaugurated by his resurrection and calling their people to accept God's offer of salvation in the days that separated them from the judgment that stood at the threshold of the world to come.

It was clear that they constituted a distinctive group of Jews, but at that time Judaism was made up of a variety of such religious groups. Beyond their participation in the history of their people, a belief in the one God who had guided their fortunes from the time of Abraham, Isaac, and Jacob, and a fidelity to the Law of Moses, there was no detailed creed or code to which all Jews were obliged to subscribe. Even the Law of Moses was interpreted in different ways. There was no "normative Judaism" in the light of which nonconformists might be branded heretical or unorthodox.

Within those parameters a broad spectrum of beliefs and attitudes was possible. Late in the first century the historian Josephus listed four such groups, or sects–Sadducees, Pharisees, Essenes, and Zealots–and there is good reason to think that there were others as well. In the Acts of the Apostles Luke was keen to present the new community as a sect like the Pharisees and Sadducees. He suggests that from early in their history they designated themselves as "the Way" and that later they were known in Jerusalem as "the Nazoreans" (Acts 24:5, 14).

The discoveries of the last fifty years, including the Dead Sea scrolls, have furnished a clearer picture of that diversity. We understand better the variety of their distinctive approaches to the Jewish religion, the attitude of each group to the Scriptures, to the Law of Moses, to the priestly leaders, the Temple, and its worship. We know more of their social composition and their organization, and we appreciate better the points of Jewish belief and practice on which they disagreed and the arguments with which each attempted to justify their claim to be the authentic Israel. We are thus better equipped to place the Jesus movement in its proper place within this spectrum of Jewish sects.

Zealots and Sadducees

Two of the groups Josephus mentions can be dealt with quite briefly. The Zealots represented the radical left wing. They were those Jews who were implacably opposed to Roman domination. Violent resistance to pagan oppressors was for them a duty arising out of their faith in God, the ruler of Israel. But it is uncertain that in the time of Jesus they constituted an organized resistance movement, much less a religious sect, and the last of them perished in the Roman siege of the fortress at Masada in 73 C.E. Nonetheless a certain Simon the Zealot is numbered as one of the Twelve (Luke 6:15), and the existence of terrorists of this kind reminds us that no Jewish religious movement could avoid adopting an attitude to Roman rule.

The Sadducees, by contrast, represented right-wing conservatism. They were the ruling class and included many of the high priests. Their leadership position brought them into frequent contact with the Roman authorities, to whom the high priest owed his office and with whom, not surprisingly, they supported a policy of peaceful coexistence. They adopted a very literal interpretation of the Scriptures, placed a premium on the Torah, or Law of Moses, among the biblical books, and rejected the body of oral tradition and interpretation that had grown up around the Torah over the centuries. They rejected, for instance, the belief in the resurrection of the dead, which was not attested in ancient writings but had originated in apocalyptic circles in the relatively recent past. Their power base was the Temple, for they controlled its worship and its revenues. With the destruction of the Temple in 70 C.E. they disappear from the pages of history.

Pharisees

Much more akin to the Jesus movement were the Pharisees. Here, if anywhere, Christians need to be reminded of the limits of the Gospels as historical sources and the way in which the Pharisees are depicted, especially in the Gospels of Matthew and John. These Gospels were written by authors who still saw themselves as Jews but whose claim to be authentic Jews was no longer recognized in the very synagogues in which they had worshiped since childhood. When they told the story of Jesus for Jewish Christians agonizing over their rejection by a Jewish leadership that was predominantly Pharisaic, those two Jewish gospel writers portrayed the Pharisees of Jesus' time with the features of the Pharisees of their own time half a century later.

The Pharisees, like Jesus, were laypeople. They had developed a particularly lay spirituality on the basis of their interpretation of the Torah. They wanted to see the kind of holiness demanded by the Torah of priests involved in Temple worship spread to the details of daily life in home and family. This entailed careful observance of Sabbaths as well as laws governing diet, purity, and tithes. They saw their role as building a hedge around the Torah, of making explicit what the letter of the Law left implicit. Some of them, living in towns and cities, gathered in a kind of small faith-support or fellowship group, or *havurah,* whose members were known as *haverim,* or fellows. They lived in towns and cities but had no formal structure, though they may well have regarded themselves as the only authentic Jews.

Carried to extremes this approach could lead to legalism and disdain of others less instructed in the niceties of religious observance, but the Pharisees were quite aware of this hazard. They were theological innovators, however, accepting that God's Law needed adaptation or new interpretation in different circumstances and that the new interpretation could be as truly Torah as the written Word of the Scriptures. They believed that God's revelation had not ceased centuries before and accepted the belief in the resurrection of the dead.

Here, then, was a body of skilled lay interpreters of the Law and the Scriptures, pioneers, in fact, of a lay spirituality. The Sadducees were installed in the Temple but the Pharisees exercised their considerable moral influence through their teaching in the local synagogues. When the era of Temple worship and sacrifice came to an end with the destruction of the Temple in Jerusalem and the Sadducee leadership had perished or been discredited, it was the Pharisees who assumed the obligation of rebuilding Judaism on the foundation of Torah and the home.

Essenes

The Jewish sect we know best is the group that produced the materials that have come to be known as the Dead Sea scrolls. Generally regarded as the Essenes of whom Josephus writes, they appear as a kind of monastic group established at Qumran, on the fringe of the desert by the Dead Sea. The library they have left behind contains extensive materials of different kinds. Practically all the books of the Jewish Scriptures were found there, many in multiple copies. There are many commentaries on the Scriptures, together with prayers and psalms they composed that are very similar to those of the Scriptures, and there are also copies of many apocalyptic books.

This material provides a very clear picture of the beliefs and organization of an apocalyptic Jewish sect that had been in existence for nearly two centuries before the time of Jesus and for the first forty years of the existence of the Jesus movement until their destruction by the Romans in 68 C.E. It is a group whose life was centered on the study of the Scriptures. Their founder, whom they called the Righteous Teacher, had left them a tradition of scriptural interpretation, which found the events of their community's history described in advance in the ancient scriptural texts.

They did this by a method of interpretation that has come to be known as a *pesher*. The Hebrew term simply means "interpretation." The pesher on Habakkuk, for instance, is a verse-by-verse explanation of the prophecy of Habakkuk written in the sixth century B.C.E., whose words are interpreted as foretelling the happenings of the history of the Qumran community five centuries later. This method enabled them to interpret world events (such as the rise of the Roman Empire) as well as events as close to home (such as the persecution of their leader by the Jerusalem priesthood) as so many steps in God's mysterious plan, soon to reach its finale in their time in a conflict between the forces of good and evil.

Apocalyptic

The term "apocalyptic" simply means "unveiling." It applies both to a kind of literature that had become popular in certain Jewish circles in the centuries immediately before and after Christ and to the characteristic ideas and beliefs which that literature expresses. In books such as the Apocalypse of Enoch, the Assumption of Moses, and the biblical book of Daniel a famous hero of the past explains his symbolic visions or dreams. These outline the stages of world history as empire succeeds empire, leading up to a crescendo that is reached in the sufferings or persecution of the writer's own time. These sufferings can only be the prelude to God's final intervention on behalf of an oppressed people, who become instruments of divine judgment on God's enemies.

Apocalyptic literature and the mind-set it expresses adopt a basically pessimistic attitude to this world, which it regards as essentially corrupt and doomed to destruction. The whole universe in its different realms–heavenly, earthly, and subterranean–is a great battleground contested by superhuman powers of good and evil locked in continual warfare. This pessimism is offset by an equal optimism about God and the covenant promise. For God, not earthly emperors, is the real master of history. It is God who is leading this present era in a mysterious way but by definite stages to a climactic action by which Yahweh's mastery will be finally asserted. Then this present world will be brought to an end, God will usher in "the world to come," where all evil powers will be vanquished. In the new age, "the world to come," God's justice and God's Law will be the uncontested guides. Apocalyptic literature was written as encouragement to persecuted and desperate people, urging them to continued fidelity and repentance in preparation for that coming judgment.

What events would serve as prelude to the end of this evil world? What manner of person would be the human instrument of God's victory? What would be the reward of the just in the world to come? These and similar questions offered ample scope to the apocalyptic imagination. Writers drew pictures of cosmic battles, heavenly courtrooms, and judgment scenes in heaven. They pictured a mysterious symbolic figure like a "son of man," or human being to whom God would delegate divine power of judgment. Confronted with the situation of martyrs whose death was simultaneously the ultimate expression of their fidelity to God and their final separation from God, they were forced to the belief in the resurrection of the dead. If God were to be true to that promise, this heroism must be rewarded by restoring to the new life of the world to come those who had laid down their life in this evil world.

Beliefs and Organization

The Essenes shared these beliefs. They regarded that divine intervention as imminent. They prepared for that moment by separation from the world and withdrawal into the desert, by dedication of all their possessions to the service of the community, by observance of a rigorous code of ethics, and at least in most cases, by renouncing marriage and family in a celibate life.

They saw themselves as the only authentic Jews. So they appropriated to themselves terms that the Scriptures applied to Israel as a whole and described themselves as the community of the new covenant, promised by the prophets, and the faithful remnant of Israel. They refused to participate in worship in the Temple in Jerusalem, which they regarded as hopelessly defiled by an illegitimate priesthood, the abandonment of traditional ways such as the ancient liturgical calendar, which they retained in their own worship, and the introduction of heathen, Hellenistic usages. It was their community itself, they believed, which had become the true Temple.

Despite their withdrawal from Jerusalem and the worship of the Temple, they attached a considerable importance to the priesthood in the organization of day-to-day affairs and in their hopes for the future. The whole community met in general assembly at Pentecost to renew the covenant. A supreme council was made up of twelve men, representatives of the tribes of Israel, and three priests. They were divided into groups of ten, each of which had a priest and another official, known as a *mebaqqer,* or supervisor, who was charged with the duties of instruction, pastoral care, and administration. They expected that God's victory would be brought about by two Messiahs, or anointed persons, one a priest, the other a Davidic king.

The Jesus Movement

The Jesus movement that came into existence in Jerusalem at Pentecost shared much in common with both Pharisees and Essenes. There was little possibility of confusing them with the Sadducean aristocracy, whose authority Jesus had threatened and who had shared in the responsibility for his death, or with the Zealots, whose violence and terrorist tactics were the antithesis of Jesus' demand for forgiveness of enemies.

They might have been taken for a Pharisaic *havurah* of one kind or another. There was variety enough among the ranks of the Pharisees, and Jesus himself had shared some of their teaching. Moreover the Pharisees were characterized by their belief in the resurrection of the dead, and the new group insisted precisely on the resurrection of the dead as the core of their belief.

They could be classed more readily as a group of urban Essenes, for there were Essenes living in the southwest section of Jerusalem. They were stamped with the same eager expectation of the end of times. The earliest Christian document we have, Paul's first letter to the Thessalonians, though written twenty years later and addressed to non-Jewish Christians in the Hellenistic world, still attests the keenness of apocalyptic expectation in that place and time. It is difficult to imagine the intensity of feeling among the original group in Jerusalem in the immediate aftermath of the appearances of the risen Jesus. Here, surely, was the greatest of God's saving acts, the finale of the history of salvation. They were living in the last days of "this world"; what remained could only be the briefest epilogue before God rang down the curtain and "the world to come" became a reality.

This similarity with the Essenes can be noticed in what we know of their organization. In Luke's story we have examples of a general assembly and of a group of twelve who represent the renewed people of God (Acts 6:2). Later Christian writings, even some epistles of Paul, talk of an official whose Greek title *episkopos* corresponds closely to that of the supervisor of Qumran. Luke mentions a number of priests who become believers (Acts 6:7), but there is no sign of a priestly leadership.

What separated them most clearly from the Essenes was the very principle on which, in a sense, they both agreed. Both groups claimed to have received from their teacher the key to the interpretation of the Scriptures. The Essenes, taught by the Righteous Teacher and others who continued the tradition he established, interpreted the Scriptures as revealing in advance the history of their community. The Jesus movement claimed to have been taught by the risen Jesus to discern the fulfillment of the Scriptures in the brief history of their own group. God's promise of the gift of the Spirit to the chosen people at the end of days had been fulfilled in the events that had brought them together, in their new-found faith and vitality, their transformation from frightened followers into courageous witnesses. Here, then, was evidence that theirs was the authentic community of the new covenant.

What set them apart from Pharisees and Essenes alike was their belief about Jesus. The Pharisees believed in a resurrection of the dead, which they expected for the future. The new group proclaimed that very resurrection as an accomplished fact and a present reality in the person of Jesus. The era of the resurrection had already begun. Not, however, according to any of the scenarios previously imagined by apocalyptic writers but in that one man. The Jesus who had been put to death God had restored to a kind of life hitherto unimaginable. In the risen Jesus "the world to come" was already with them.

4 The Message in Jerusalem

Luke's Picture

In the first five chapters of the Acts of the Apostles Luke paints in glowing colors a picture of the Jesus movement in its earliest days. He shows us a group of men and women gathered in prayerful expectation in Jerusalem after the resurrection. We watch the explosion of faith at Pentecost when the inner conviction and joy of their resurrection faith came to expression in charismatic utterance and public preaching (Acts 2:14-40). We admire the transformation of Peter and John and the apostles as they testify, preach, work miracles, and argue with the leaders of their people (Acts 3–5). We catch a glimpse of one of the community's heroes, Barnabas, model of generosity and sharing of possessions (Acts 4:36-37), and two of its black sheep, the deceitful Ananias and Sapphira (Acts 5:1-12). In a series of cameos and tableaux Luke pictures a community united around the apostles in prayer and thanksgiving whose sharing of possessions creates a space where poverty and human need are eliminated (Acts 4:32-35).

It is not hard to recognize this picture as an idealization of a past era for Christians of Luke's own time. The early days of the Jerusalem community become the "golden age" of the Church, a model for Gentile Christians half a century later and a standard by which to measure their own age. In fact, it is the features of the authentic Christian community of every age that Luke delineates in his well-known summary: "They devoted themselves to the teaching of the apostles, the fellowship, the breaking of bread and the prayers" (Acts 2:42).

How much precise historical information he has incorporated into this picture and the extent of the sources he draws on, however, is uncertain. The work of redaction critics on Luke's Gospel has revealed the characteristic ways in which he adapts the materials he utilizes in his first volume, namely the Gospel of Mark and the Q document. We approach his second volume, then, aware that some elements of his picture are likely to be attributed to Luke's distinctive literary style and his special theological interests rather than to factual historical information at his disposal. It is possible to distinguish to some extent the traditions underlying the story in Acts from the pictorial setting in which Luke places them and assess their historical value against whatever other sources are available. Such is the facility with which Luke incorporates his sources into his own work, however, that this is not an easy task and its results often remain problematic.

We can ask, for example, whether the earliest proclamation of the resurrection was so neatly and thoroughly centralized in Jerusalem as Luke makes it in his Pentecost story, or whether it may not have happened even before then in other places in which the risen Lord appeared. Luke knew that there were stories of such appearances in Galilee, since they are referred to by Mark, on whose narrative he was drawing in his own Gospel, but he confined his account to those appearances in or near Jerusalem. By so doing he made Jerusalem the center of the history of salvation; Jesus "goes up" to Jerusalem and then "goes up" from Jerusalem to heaven, while the Gospel goes out from Jerusalem to the ends of the earth. In his first volume no appearances in Galilee distract from the centrality of Jerusalem and the Temple where the story begins and ends.

In view of these clear signs of arrangement on Luke's part, his concentration on Jerusalem to the exclusion of other places, it is reasonable to think that the message of the resurrection was also proclaimed in other places where disciples had experienced the risen Jesus alive and present among them and that groups of believers sprang up there as well as in Jerusalem. Some scholars have thought that such communities existed in Galilee, where the risen Jesus appeared to the disciples, even though there is little evidence in the Gospels to support this conjecture. There is evidence in the Gospels, however, of other groups of Jewish believers in Palestine whose origins cannot simply be traced to the pentecostal preaching in Jerusalem but may lie in the preaching of disciples of Jesus in other places.

The group that reassembled in Jerusalem was not large. It included Peter and the rest of the Twelve—with the awful exception of Judas—and the women disciples. Luke's brief catalogue includes the mother of Jesus and his brothers, and there is good reason to accept this detail as historical recollection (Acts 1:13). It was, then, from this small group of uprooted Galilean disciples together with his widowed mother and relatives, one of whom, James, was later to become leader of the Jerusalem community, that the Jesus movement began in Jerusalem.

Witness and Kerygma

The core group, whom Luke simply designates as "the apostles" and usually identifies with "the Twelve," was responsible for a function known well before Luke as "the testimony of the resurrection" (Acts 4:33). This was the bedrock on which the existence of the community rested. To the people of Jerusalem these witnesses testified that Jesus of Nazareth, with whom they had lived and who had been crucified, was alive, that it was indeed the Jesus of Nazareth they knew who had appeared to them. Nor could the testimony of these unlettered persons be shaken by any kind of intimidation. It was confirmed by the surprising change that had taken place in their lives, not only by the conviction carried by their charismatic utterance but by the new-found courage and steadfastness that authenticated their claim that the new age had arrived and God's Spirit was poured out on the chosen people.

This basic testimony, or witness, of the core group was elaborated by the apostles and preachers in public proclamation, or what the New Testament writers call "kerygma," a Greek term that designates both the activity of the herald and the message he proclaimed. The term they chose shows us how that function was understood. They were not teachers, rabbis explaining the Law of Moses, or itinerant philosophers expounding a new way of life. Like John the Baptist proclaiming a baptism of penance (Mark 1:4) and Jesus himself proclaiming the gospel of the kingdom (Matt 4:23), their task was that of heralds commissioned to give maximum publicity to a message from God. That message was neither a new creed nor a new code of conduct nor a new cult but the proclamation of the climactic event in God's dealings with the chosen people and God's final offer of salvation to them.

In what terms was the Christian message first proclaimed? Did the first preachers simply proclaim the coming of the kingdom in the same terms as Jesus had? If not, how did they differ? Is it possible to recover the original form of their preaching or at least the kind of pattern gradually established by regular repetition? It would surely be invaluable to recover the elements the earliest Christians thought were indispensable in the presentation of the good news; here, if ever, would be a sure guide for the faith and preaching of Christians of later ages, the kind of universal catechism that would be acceptable to all Christians.

Half a century ago a great deal of scholarly energy was expended in that task. Scholars turned once again to the pages of Luke and Paul. By analyzing the common features in the speeches of Peter (Acts 2:14-39; 3:12-26; 4:8-12; 5:29-32; 10:34-43) and Paul (Acts 13:16-41) to Jewish audiences they hoped to discover a fixed pattern in the primitive preaching. This outline was considered to be reinforced and extended by a study of elements in Paul's letters that seemed to indicate the way he had preached when first he evangelized his churches.

Their results have not been generally accepted. First, because those sources do not take us back far enough. Luke followed the custom of writers of his era who composed speeches for their heroes that were appropriate to the occasion, so there is much more of Luke in the sample sermons he placed in the mouths of Peter and Paul than there is of those earliest preachers themselves. Moreover, even in those Lucan samples there are signs that different presentations could be employed and that the presentation of the kerygma always depended to some degree on the circumstances of the precise audience addressed and the insight and rhetorical skill of the individual preacher.

When due allowance has been made for these variations, however, some elements remain constant. The earliest preachers proclaimed the resurrection of Jesus and called for commitment to him in order to benefit by God's promises to the chosen people. When Jesus preached "the good news of God" during his lifetime, he proclaimed the advent of the kingdom of God present in his ministry and person and summoned God's people to a radical change of attitude and faith in the God whom he revealed. The difference between the proclamation of Jesus and that of these early preachers can be summarized in a well-known phrase–where Jesus had proclaimed the advent of the kingdom of God these first preachers proclaimed the resurrection of Jesus. In the new situation brought about by God in raising Jesus from the dead, the call to faith was a summons to commitment to the risen Jesus, which demanded accepting him as leader and adopting his "way" in the new community he had brought into being.

Paul was to write of the paradoxical ways of God, who offered salvation to Jews and Gentiles alike through "the folly of our kerygma" (1 Cor 1:21). He was not saying that salvation was mediated by correct presentation of the truths of faith or doctrinal orthodoxy. It is clear that God's saving action is not chained to verbal accuracy or the exact repetition of one set pattern or formula. Nor is it, for that matter, confined to the initial preaching that sparks faith into flame, nor even to the activity of an individual preacher, however gifted. Proclamation is as much a function of the whole community as it is of an individual preacher or teacher; in its worship, for example, the whole community "proclaims the death of the Lord until he comes" (1 Cor 11:26). What ultimately makes of that proclamation "the power of God for salvation" (Rom 1:16) is the power of the Spirit with which the risen Jesus endows the community he leads and the proclaimer he empowers.

Metanoia

Just as the proclamation of Jesus was a summons to conversion so, too, was the proclamation of those first preachers. Kerygma was a summons to metanoia, the favored New Testament term for a radical change of heart or mind-set. What kind of attitudinal change did this demand of an observant Jew, a member of one of their audiences in Jerusalem?

The first and indispensable change of attitude was to the preachers themselves. This movement had started in the lifetime of Jesus when his disciples had accepted Jesus and his message; it was to continue after his death when other Jews accepted these men and women as trustworthy witnesses of a well-nigh unbelievable happening rather than as a bunch of misguided Galilean enthusiasts.

Acceptance of their message meant a change in attitude to Jesus of a kind that is difficult to imagine. Those Jewish audiences were called to accept that a man condemned by the highest court of their people as a criminal was indeed the one sent by God to lead the chosen people into the new age, that a man crucified by the Romans as an insurrectionist brought with him the fulfillment of every promise God had ever made to them. Some members of those audiences in Jerusalem had played, perhaps, an active part in the death of Jesus. Others, surely by far the majority, had been passive spectators or simply members of an apathetic public. Though the earliest preachers were reticent about the details of Jesus' shameful death, they were forthright in taxing their audience with their guilt and calling them to repentance for "rejecting the Holy and the Righteous One" and "killing the Author of Life" (Acts 3:14f.).

A change in attitude to Jesus brought with it a change in attitude to God. The resurrection had shown that the God of Israel was no longer simply the God of Abraham, Isaac, and

Jacob but God the "Abba," or Father, of Jesus. Never during his life had God been seen so clearly allied with Jesus as in the act of raising him from the dead. In the new era begun by the resurrection God's action remained allied to the same Jesus, who remained as a palpable presence, however mysterious, in the community of his disciples.

However radical this change of attitude may have been, it certainly did not represent a change of religion. This was a Jewish message, proclaimed by Jews to fellow Jews. It was not a call to abandon their traditional faith for something entirely different. It presented no threat to traditional Jewish morality or belief. It spoke about the God of Abraham, Isaac, and Jacob and claimed that he had acted again and definitively on behalf of his chosen people. In raising Jesus from the dead he had performed the most wonderful of all the mighty deeds that constituted that people's history.

To what extent this conversion may have alienated those Jewish believers from their own kith and kin it is hard to say. Membership in a new sect did not make a Jew a renegade or a heretic. Other Jews may well have seen their joining this new Jewish group as a change of allegiance from one Jewish sect to another, nothing more than those Pharisees and priests were doing who were joining his community. Some, perhaps, suffered ostracism from families firmly entrenched in their allegiance to another sect. Others doubtless shared their faith with their fellows in home and synagogue and won more members to the new community.

The Q Community

It is possible to study the way the message was presented to Jews in other parts of Palestine. A literary hypothesis widely accepted by scholars assigns the gospel material shared by Matthew and Luke but lacking in Mark to another source on which they both draw labeled Q, probably from the German word *Quelle,* meaning "source." It is commonly thought that this was a collection written in Greek of sayings of Jesus with virtually none of the narrative connections that make the Gospels a continuous story. The document itself cannot be placed at an early date, but it is regarded as the production of a Jewish community existing in Palestine from as early as the period from 30 C.E. to 50 C.E. An analysis of its contents shows emphases in its presentation of the message significantly different from those of the Jerusalem community as Luke presents it.

The community's guiding spirits were wandering prophets, possibly disciples of Jesus during his ministry, who continued to preach his message after the resurrection. These charismatic figures had made a complete break with their own homes, families, and possessions to preach the message of the kingdom, while other Christians who had settled in towns and villages provided them support. Study of the Q materials shows them to be apocalyptic enthusiasts living in imminent expectation of the return of Jesus, the Son of Man, instrument of God's judgment.

In their preaching, they believed, the voice of Jesus present in their community was being heard; no distinction was made between the words of Jesus and the words of prophets who spoke in his name. They repeated Jesus' proclamation of the kingdom by elaborating on the sayings of Jesus, but their materials place little emphasis on his death and resurrection. The emphasis of these preachers was on an urgent call to repent in view of judgment still to come, indeed due at any moment, rather than a proclamation of the kingdom inaugurated through the resurrection.

The First Christian Creeds

From the earliest days of the community's existence its faith found verbal expression in simple slogans, or confessions. Probably the simplest of them was "Jesus is Messiah." Despite the reluctance of Jesus to accept that title during his lifetime, his death and resurrection had clarified its meaning beyond any possibility of confusion with dreams of Jewish national ascendancy. God had indeed fulfilled the promise to raise up a leader like King David. The resurrection was the anointing and enthronement that established Jesus as king exercising God's power to save this people.

During his lifetime people had addressed him with the common Aramaic term, *mare,* a deferential form of address to a superior but one with a very wide range of meanings, depending on the measure of superiority of the person addressed. It ranged from a respectful "sir" through various degrees of sovereignty all the way to the title "Lord" for the divine majesty of God. This range of meaning made it an excellent vehicle to respect the mystery that surrounded Jesus. However vaguely sensed and haltingly articulated during his life, that mystery, too, had been clarified by God in the resurrection, which had shown how thoroughly God had endowed Jesus with God's own sovereignty. The prophet Joel, speaking of the end of times, had promised salvation to "those who call on the name of the Lord," the God of Israel (Joel 2:32). The followers of Jesus professed their belief that "Jesus is Lord" and identified themselves as "those who call on the name of the Lord" (cf. Acts 2:21; 9:14, 21).

These early Christian creeds, or "symbols," encapsulated not only the message of the preachers but also the response of the believers. The emphasis of the message fell on an act of God, something that *God* had done *to Jesus* for the salvation of the chosen people. Its terms were thoroughly Jewish and acceptable to the most rigid monotheism. It clearly did not identify Jesus with the Father to whom he prayed during his life on earth but spoke of a transformation brought about in Jesus by God who "made him Lord and Christ" (Acts 2:36), recipient and dispenser of all God's saving power.

From the beginning faith found expression in language that is symbolic, evocative, touching as many levels as possible in the humanity of believers. It spoke to their minds, certainly, but it stirred the heart and fired imagination, liberating affectivity and lodging as deep as the wellsprings of the subconscious. This is the language used by those who share an experience, not of those who observe it from the outside. It struggles to express a relationship between the believer and God present in the risen Jesus.

Symbols always defy exhaustive intellectual analysis. The mysterious reality they reveal has always depths to plumb untouched by any single generation, even the one from whose immediate experience they were born. For that first generation the symbols "Messiah" and "Lord" evoked the mystery, the dynamism, and the majesty of the risen Jesus, which they experienced and expressed in their passionate commitment to Jesus and his cause, the kingdom of God. They proclaimed the absolute claim of Jesus on their loyalty and God's absolute guarantee of continuing presence in the risen Jesus.

5 The Community at Worship

The Jewish Tradition

It was only natural that the first Jewish believers in Jesus should continue to pray and worship God in the traditional Jewish prayers and practices that Jesus had learned from his parents in their family home and from his people in the village synagogue in Nazareth and in which he had shared so often with his disciples during his ministry.

From earliest childhood he had been accustomed to the morning and evening recitation of the great confession of Jewish faith known to this day, by the Hebrew word with which it begins, *as the Shema:* "Hear O Israel, the Lord our God is one Lord." This was linked with the commandment "you shall love the Lord your God with all your heart, and with all your soul, and with all your might" (Deut 6:4-5). At home he had learned from Joseph and Mary the prayers of blessing for bread and wine that made the family meal itself a prayer. Morning, noon, and night he had recited the traditional Jewish blessings.

He shared in the regular routine of Jewish worship in the simple surroundings of a village synagogue. The heart of this worship was the Torah. Jesus imbibed the faith of his people from the round of readings and reflection on the Scriptures, prayer, and acclamation. He learned the message of the prophets and the psalms, Israel's sacred songs, the texts that were to help him discern his own vocation and support him in his distress. During his ministry synagogue worship provided a natural context for his proclamation of the message of the kingdom.

As an adult he joined his people on pilgrimage to Jerusalem for the three great pilgrimage feasts that kept alive the memory of God's acts of salvation for Israel. At Passover they recalled the deliverance from Egypt, at Pentecost the gift of the covenant at Sinai, and at Tabernacles God's care for them in the sojourn in the desert. By the recitation of the story and the symbolic ritual of the feast, its processions, songs, sacrifices, and festive meals, its reenactment of the events of the past, each generation "remembered" the deeds by which God had brought them into existence and sustained them as a people in the present. Through this memorial those past events became a dynamic influence to shape the present. Each generation was touched anew by God's power as if they had undergone the initial experience of their forebears.

Not all devout Jews, however, joined enthusiastically in Temple worship. The Essenes at Qumran, as we have seen, had withdrawn completely into the prayer and worship of their desert community. Other Greek-speaking Jews from the Diaspora, too, showed little interest in the Temple. In the Gospels Jesus is both at home with his people in the Temple, teaching in its courts, and at the same time a stern prophetic critic of the priestly leaders who had made the Temple their power base. His symbolic cleansing of the Temple (Mark 11:15-17) and the enigmatic saying about its end (Mark 14:58; John 2:19) show that for him, as for the prophet Jeremiah, the Temple was of no value if it did not serve its God-given purpose.

The Prayer of Jesus

The Gospels testify regularly to the prayerfulness of Jesus even if they provide us with little by way of formulas he used. When asked by a scribe about the greatest commandment in the Law he harks back to that basic Israelite creed so regularly recited as the key to all the commandments (Mark 12:29-30). One of the few prayer formulas the evangelists place on his lips is a typical form of Jewish prayer, a *berakah,* or blessing prayer.

"I bless you, Father, Lord of heaven and earth, for hiding these things from the wise and clever and revealing them to mere children" (Matt 11:25-27) proclaims God's wonderful and entirely paradoxical action in the lives of unlettered folk who have accepted his message and the incomprehension of those who might have been expected to welcome him, the religious teachers and leaders.

Though Jesus used the same prayer forms it was clear to his disciples that something set him apart from other Jews, even Jewish teachers of prayer like John the Baptist, the Pharisees, and the Essenes. The Gospels recall some of the important lessons he taught his disciples about prayer and especially the pattern he gave them for the prayer of a disciple (Luke 11:1-13). In the Our Father the central themes of his proclamation of the kingdom are transposed into petitionary prayer, but the petitions themselves do not differ greatly in form from contemporary Jewish prayers; what is most distinctive is the initial address to God as *Abba.*

The meals he shared with them were enclosed by moments of prayer and blessing, simple celebrations of God's goodness conveyed by the gifts of food and drink and the joy of human fellowship. To share another's table was to share in the blessing pronounced over the bread, to be assured of peaceful relations and even a kind of kinship. Never was the presence of the kingdom of God more dramatically proclaimed than when Jesus invited sinful, nonreligious people and outcasts to share a meal with him or when he shared a meal to which they invited him (Luke 5:29; 15:1). In those meals the fellowship portrayed in prophetic images of the banquet to which God invited the chosen people (Isa 25:6-8) became a present reality in the humble human circumstances of Palestinian hospitality.

The Jesus Movement

Luke's picture of the pentecostal community in Jerusalem depicts one united group uniformly participating in the regular liturgical observances in the Temple, its prayers, sacrifices, and feasts. As we shall see not all the first believers shared such an enthusiastic attitude to the Temple, but whatever there was of diffidence or reserve in the attitude of Jesus to the Temple does not seem to have deterred at least one group of those first believers from Temple worship. There were some, Luke also points out, who continued to join other Jews in Greek-speaking synagogues in Jerusalem, where their enthusiastic faith in Jesus as Messiah, but probably even more their critical attitude to the Temple, was eventually to arouse strong opposition and the persecution that led to the death of Stephen (Acts 6:8–7:60).

It was in their own homes rather than in the Temple or the synagogue that their distinctive forms of prayer and worship took shape. In these gatherings their wonder at what had happened to them in the resurrection and their expectation of its finale in a return of Jesus surely soon to come were given free rein. Here they felt most acutely the mysterious presence of their risen Lord, entered finally and fully into God's world but just as really present and active among them by his power or Spirit. This it was that produced in them the joy that came of faith affirmed and expectation heightened practically beyond the limits of articulate expression and voiced in ecstatic speech. Decades later Greek-speaking Christians were still using in their worship the Aramaic acclamation Maranatha, "Our Lord, come," which had first resounded in those gatherings in Jerusalem (1 Cor 16:22). It shows us something of the intensity of their yearning for the return of Jesus and the end of this age.

It was in worship, too, that their characteristic approach to the Scriptures was born. It was essentially the same as the *pesher* technique in use by the Essenes. When, as they claimed, the risen Jesus "opened their minds to understand the scriptures" (Luke 24:45), then psalms and prophets spoke to them of what had happened in the resurrection of Jesus and its overflow on them. Psalms that had been used originally in the enthronement of Israel's kings and that had come over the centuries to express the hope of Israel for the future triumph of an heir of David they now found fulfilled in the resurrection, which was the exaltation of Jesus to share God's power, his enthronement as God's viceroy, and his victory over his enemies (Acts 2:34-36). The transformation that had overtaken them they found predicted in the promise of the prophet Joel, made four hundred years before, that God would lavish the Spirit on the chosen people at the end of time (Acts 2:17-21).

In their worship they sang the same songs as other Jews, but psalms and canticles they had previously prayed and sung with Jesus during his life to praise God for wonderful deeds in the past and to plead for divine assistance assumed a new and deeper meaning when sung in the presence of the same Jesus risen from the dead. They also developed songs and prayers of their own, following traditional Jewish models such as the psalms and canticles of typical Old Testament figures. The hymns Luke was later to incorporate into his story of the infancy of Jesus and place on the lips of Zechariah and Mary, the Benedictus and the Magnificat (Luke 1:46-55, 68-79), may well be products of this early activity. It is likely that the tradition of composing hymns to Jesus, which is clearly evidenced a decade later in communities outside Palestine, had its origins in the early Jerusalem community.

Baptism

Two rituals further distinguished the Jesus movement from other Jewish communities. The first was its rite of initiation. Those who accepted the message in faith and sought admission to the community were admitted through the symbolic ritual of baptism. Conversion was not something that could be confined to the sanctuary of the individual conscience; it called for outward expression in a bodily, public, communitarian ceremony.

Some of them had been baptized before by John in the waters of the Jordan. Converted by his preaching, they had professed their repentance in that rite of purification from a sinful past and their preparation for God's coming judgment. Jesus himself had joined his people at the Jordan. In his acceptance of John's baptism he manifested his solidarity with that sinful but purified people and committed himself to his vocation. God's response to this dedication of Jesus to his life's work was his "anointing with the Holy Spirit and power" (Acts 10:38), the gift of the Spirit that consecrated him for his prophetic ministry.

It is likely that Jesus baptized people during his ministry, following in the steps of John, but one became his disciple not by undergoing the ritual of baptism but by acceptance of his personal invitation. People who listened to his preaching entered the kingdom by accepting his message and undertaking the kind of life it demanded. After the resurrection, however, that traditional Jewish rite of purification became the natural expression of the conversion effected by the missioners who preached in his name. No longer a rite of preparation for the future like the baptism of John, it was now a rite of passage into a new world already opened up by the risen Jesus and evident in the transformation of the believers brought about by the gift of the Spirit. From a baptism of water it had become a baptism of water and the Holy Spirit and was the usual vehicle through which the gift of the Spirit was either confirmed or conferred, a rite of initiation into the new community of believers.

They were baptized "into the name of the Lord Jesus" (Acts 8:16; 19:5). Scholars have found the precise background and meaning of that phrase elusive. What is clear is that it distinguished this rite from similar rituals of other Jewish groups, such as the Essenes and the disciples of John the Baptist. It connected a familiar ritual with the community's experience of the risen Jesus, by whose representative it was administered and to whose discipleship it summoned its recipient. That archaic phrase is the first link in the long chain of reflection on the significance of the symbolic ritual whose earliest links are to be found in the pages of the New Testament.

The Breaking of Bread

The second distinctive ritual of the Jesus movement in Jerusalem was "the breaking of bread" (Acts 2:42). This, too, took place neither in the Temple nor in the synagogue but in the home. It was a sacred meal in which they shared the kind of fellowship that marked the meals Jesus ate during his ministry with his disciples and with people of all kinds. These meals had been much more than simple secular occasions. Jesus had made them sacred moments when, as host, he had broken bread and recited the blessing over it, proclaiming, praising, and thanking God for these gifts. On festive occasions particularly, the initial blessing of bread and final thanksgiving over wine wrapped the intervening moments of human communication in prayer. The bread that was distributed was something more than physical nourishment; it was the bearer of the blessing of God pronounced over it, the blessing that created the special human fellowship of the table.

Those meals had culminated in the meal he ate with his disciples on the eve of his death. The Last Supper does not stand alone as a unique gesture of Jesus like a solitary peak rising out of a featureless plain; it is rather the last of a series of meals, the summit of a mountain range. It brings into sharper focus the action that has been taking place in them all, the work of God creating a new fellowship, that of the kingdom. It picks out the part played by Jesus, whose words over bread and wine charged them with all the power of the self-sacrificing love and service that was about to be shown in blinding clarity on Calvary.

It is not certain that Jesus' last supper was a traditional Jewish paschal meal. Though the evangelists Matthew, Mark, and Luke certainly present it as such, the narrative of John would exclude that possibility. It is possible that Jesus heightened the significance of his final meal by comparing it with the paschal meal that other Jews would soon be eating.

The early gatherings for "the breaking of bread" continued the Jewish tradition of the memorial, the remembrance of God's saving actions by ritual recall. The great deed the first believers recalled was no longer deliverance from Egypt or the gift of the covenant of Sinai or God's providence for the chosen people in the desert. The event in the history of their community that they recalled, the deliverance offered to them in their day, the covenant renewed in their meal, was the new covenant,

God's final offer of fellowship achieved in the death and resurrection of Jesus.

The symbolic action of breaking of bread was accompanied by the recitation of the events it recalled, those of the Last Supper–its preparation and aftermath in his sufferings and death. It is in these early gatherings for worship that the origin of the passion story is to be placed. Those early recitations, many times repeated over the decades and adapted to the circumstances of different cultural groups, were to provide the stuff from which the evangelists wove the story of the passion in their written Gospels.

Other Jewish groups of the time attached a special religious significance to meals they took together. Groups of Pharisees met for meals to reinforce their religious dedication to the observance of the Torah. The Essenes shared meals that were blessed by a priest and that looked forward to the day when God would send them two Messiahs, one a priest, the other a king, to preside over the messianic banquet with them. What distinguished the breaking of bread and the worship of the new groups was the place they assigned to Jesus. In their acclamations, their prayer addressed to Jesus, the hymns of praise for what God had done and continued to do in their midst through Jesus–in all these they were something other than Pharisees or Essenes or other Jewish sects. They were a Jesus movement.

The Language of Worship

Like every other Jew, Jesus worshiped the God of Abraham, Isaac, and Jacob, the God, that is, whom those patriarchs worshiped, the guiding power recognized by Jews as alone presiding over the origins of their people and every moment of its history. During Jesus' life his disciples joined him in this worship, and he invited them to address God familiarly in the term that clearly marked his own feeling for God, "Abba," Father. The Jesus movement, the original disciples of Jesus and other Jews who accepted their preaching and joined their community, continued to worship that same one and only God. But what had happened in their time showed that the God who worked such wonders in the history of their forebears had brought that history to its climax by raising Jesus from the dead.

Now the God of Abraham, Isaac, and Jacob stood revealed as "the God and Father of Our Lord Jesus Christ," the God, that is, whom Jesus had indeed worshiped but who had finally shown himself so much a Father to Jesus as to deliver him from death and invest him with all the power with which God had not only guided the history of the chosen people in the past but had brought their new community into existence. The God who had been present and active among them in the visible humanity of Jesus in his earthly career remained present among them after his resurrection in the same humanity, no longer visible but a real and dynamic even if mysterious presence.

From as early a time as the New Testament records help us to reach, and this is practically to the earliest years of the Jesus movement, those first believers can be seen praying to God and also praying to Jesus, whom God had established as their Lord. They celebrated what God had done and continued to do through Jesus in psalms and hymns and acclamations. They saw no conflict between their faith in Jesus as Lord and Messiah and their Jewish belief in one God, and no other Jewish group accused them of apostasy from their common faith on this account.

6 Prophets and Teachers

Israel's Prophets and Teachers

The great prophets whom Israel remembered were divinely appointed spokesmen who kept alive its mission as God's chosen people by spelling out the demands of the covenant in the changing social and political circumstances of their history. Over the centuries the prophets constantly challenged them to live up to their vocation. The whole people they rebuked for assuming the ways and worship of the pagans. The rich and powerful they condemned for the injustice and oppression that deprived the poor of their rightful share in Israel's inheritance. Priests and people alike they castigated for a soulless worship that was so much empty show and a mindless complacency in the Temple, as if that monument was an automatic assurance of God's protection.

The prophets were the major channel of divine revelation. They had visions that introduced them into God's heavenly court and gave them insight into God's mysterious plans. They proclaimed God's message in oracles of many kinds, promises of salvation and threats of judgment, woes on sinful Israel and assurances of God's fidelity to the covenant. At times they served a divine summons on Israel, calling it to contend with God in court. In times of national danger and near extinction they kept alive their people's hope by predictions of deliverance, at other times they called them to repentance in preparation for the coming of the Day of the Lord. At times they acted out their message in striking symbolic actions that communicated more effectively than words.

A significant change took place after the Exile. The activity of the prophets took on new forms, especially the written form we know as apocalyptic literature. At the same time God's revelation through the Law given to Moses, now codified in the written Torah, came to pride of place as the center of Jewish life. This was the era of the scribe, the specialist in the Law. Different schools of interpretation of the written Torah formed around famous teachers or rabbis. Groups like the Pharisees devoted themselves to close study and accurate observance of the written Torah but canonized as well the body of oral interpretation that grew up around it. The study of the Torah became an act of worship, and whole communities like the Essenes at Qumran devoted their lives to this study.

Jesus as Prophet and Teacher

The Gospels show that ordinary people classed Jesus spontaneously as a prophet (Mark 6:15; 8:28). In the themes and manner of his preaching, his striking symbolic gestures, and his characteristic lifestyle they recognized the same prophetic Spirit that had driven the great prophets of the past and John the Baptist in their own time.

Like Micah, Jesus called people to the practice of love and justice rather than the externals of religion (Mic 6:6-8; Matt 23:23-28). Like Amos, he decried the hypocrisy of priests and leaders (Amos 5:21-27; Mark 3:5; 7:1f.). Like Jeremiah, he foretold the destruction of the Temple and of Jerusalem (Jer 15:5-9; Mark 13). From Jesus God's people heard once again the prophetic warnings and threats, the woes and promises that accompanied his call to conversion in view of God's impending judgment.

The same prophetic inspiration was evident in the striking symbolic actions that offered living images of the kingdom and enabled people to feel its presence in their own experience. In his healings and exorcisms God's mastery over evil was asserted

(Luke 11:20); in the meals Jesus shared with sinners God's sinful people were gathered together in reconciliation (Mark 2:15-17). In the choice of the Twelve the renewed people of God was established in the symbolic persons of its patriarchs and leaders (Matt 19:28); in the purification of the Temple he declared the end of the current form of worship (Mark 11:15-17).

The sayings of Jesus show that he, too, envisioned his mission as prophet of God's coming kingdom. He was conscious of a divine commission, of being "sent" by God (Mark 9:37). His rejection by the people with whom he grew up in Nazareth was part of the pattern of the career of the prophet (Mark 6:4). Conscious of the violent fate of the prophets of the past, he saw himself as the last of the long line of those delivered up to death by their own people (Luke 13:33-34).

One of the titles most frequently ascribed to Jesus in the Gospels is that of "teacher" (e.g. Mark 4:38; 9:38). To most Jews of his time he must have seemed like one more itinerant rabbi followed from village to village by a group of disciples. People in his own village knew that he had never undergone any formal training or served such an apprenticeship himself (Mark 6:2). Others wondered how he had acquired such authority (Mark 1:22).

It is clear that Jesus shared a great deal in common with other Jewish teachers. Even though the Gospels show him engaged in debate with other teachers on issues where he differed strongly from them (e.g. Mark 10:2-9; 12:18-27), with all of them he shared the fundamental Jewish assumption that the Scriptures were the Word of God, God's basic manner of address to the chosen people. With much of their ethical teaching he was in complete agreement; on most issues in which Jewish teachers disagreed he shared the view of the Pharisees. The way he interpreted the Scriptures, too, was customary with Jewish teachers. He deduced the meaning of the text and applied it to current circumstances in ways already listed methodically by the great teacher Hillel. Like the Essene teachers at Qumran, he found in the Scriptures the meaning of what was happening in his own world and his own life.

His teaching methods, too, were typical of Jewish teachers of his time. He was fond of short, striking sayings, epigrams that stuck fast in the memory. He countered a question with another question. He used proverbs, parables, and paradox to tease the imagination and challenge understanding. He used hyperbole, wild exaggeration, and irony to capsize a common way of understanding and open up a new way of understanding life.

What set Jesus apart from other teachers was the focus of his message, his concentration on the kingdom of God, and his unprecedented claim that all that Israel hoped would come about at the end of time was happening then and there in the course of his ministry. Other Jewish teachers employed the image of God as king as one illustration among many in their exposition of the Law of Moses; for Jesus this was the heart of his proclamation. God was finally asserting sovereignty in a world where God's word and will seemed generally disregarded, definitively establishing in that world the order intended in its creation. Unlike other teachers, Jesus sought no precedent for his message in traditional teaching. He claimed to know what the will of God was by intuition; while he affirmed the Mosaic Law as the will of God he did not hesitate to declare what God's intention was in giving the Law. He claimed the ability to rescind the letter of the Law in order to reestablish God's own intention in creation (Mark 10:5-9).

From Kerygma to Teaching

The proclamation of the kerygma brought into existence a community consisting of a number of separate groups of Jews who differed in significant ways but were unified by their belief that God had established Jesus as Messiah by raising him from the dead. They had heeded the call of the preachers to faith and metanoia; they had been initiated into a community of believers and shared in its worship. This was only the first step on a lifelong journey. Their new-found faith needed nurturing by a process of continuing instruction, which took place during worship and at other times as well. This was the task of the community's teachers.

Faith is always in search of understanding. Their first need was to grasp the meaning of their experience. How was the transformation they had undergone to be explained? How could they account for the release of the strange and unexpected energy that characterized the Jesus movement? Then they needed to explore the practical details of metanoia. Despite their belief in the imminent end of this world, their change of heart had to be embodied in the details of daily life in their social, economic, and political environment.

The need for systematic instruction was heightened by the growth of the community. Luke's figures of thousands of people baptized after each of Peter's speeches are surely inflated, but a steady stream of Jewish believers were convinced by the proclamation of the preachers and confirmed by the witness of the community's life. Many of these knew little about Jesus' teaching about the kingdom of God and had at best a sketchy knowledge of the course of his life and the events that had led to his death.

New questions arose from the response of Jewish audiences to the missionary preachers and from the daily contact of new believers with their fellow Jews in family and synagogue. The basic question encountered by preachers and believers alike was that of the crucified Messiah. How could a Jew seriously accept Jesus of Nazareth, a man condemned as a criminal by the highest and holiest court of their people, as Israel's Messiah? So poor a leader had he proved that it was a follower he had personally chosen who had turned informer and betrayed him for money. Even the manner of his death by crucifixion showed him as somebody accursed by God (Deut 21:23).

The majority of their hearers remained unconvinced. Parents and children, friends and even spouses, considered them as deluded fanatics. They had to find ways of defending their belief against this hostile criticism, to show that their message was consistent with Israel's traditional faith and God's ways of dealing with the chosen people in their history. The resurrection of Jesus, the enigma of his shameful death, and the unbelief of so many Jews had all to be shown as part of God's paradoxical pattern.

Searching the Scriptures

Their quest for understanding and for answers to these questions began in the Scriptures. Jewish teachers trained in the scribal schools and perhaps in the methods of the Essenes returned to the texts they already knew so well and found new meaning in them in the light of Easter and Pentecost. The New Testament shows us groups engaged in this "searching the Scriptures" (e.g., Acts 28:24-28), and we can find their favorite proof texts in its pages. Scholars have unraveled some of the stages in the development of this early Christian theology and apologetics. Though the results of their researches are usually no better than probable reconstructions, they have shown that those early Christian teachers returned many times to the same texts and that answers to these questions did not come overnight.

They presented the resurrection as God's speedy vindication of the claims of Jesus, the manifestation of his status as Messiah, and the inauguration of the messianic kingdom. What had happened to them they interpreted as the gift of the Spirit promised to all God's people at the end of times, now imparted as the result of Jesus' triumph. Their acceptance of God's gift offered in the kerygma constituted them as the authentic covenant community of the final age.

They pointed to the resurrection as the literal fulfillment of God's promise to "raise up" a prophet like Moses (Acts 3:22; Deut 18:15). They drew on acknowledged messianic texts such as the psalm already used by Jesus in controversy with the scribes (Mark 12:35-37; Ps 110:1) and psalms that spoke of the adoption of the Messiah as Son of God in his enthronement at God's right hand (Acts 13:33; Ps 2:7). The resurrection was God's answer to the trust of the "holy one" who prayed to be delivered from death and corruption (Acts 2:25-28; Ps 16:8-11).

Another psalm helped connect the exaltation of the Messiah with the gift of the Spirit (Acts 2:33; Ps 110:1), and a prophecy of Hosea concerning God's deliverance "on the third day" probably forms the basis of the creedal statement that "he rose again on the third day according to the Scriptures" (1 Cor 15:4; Hos 6:2).

It was much harder to find a positive value in the ignominy of Jesus' death. For the early preachers the death of Jesus was the result of the terrible no of the people of Jerusalem to God's final offer of salvation. The crucifixion was something well-nigh incomprehensible, something of which one could only say that it must, somehow, have formed part of "the definite plan and foreknowledge of God" (Acts 2:23).

Further reflection on the Scriptures showed the flaws in the accepted picture of a Messiah achieving glorious triumphs in this world. The Scriptures showed that God's work had often been achieved through leaders judged insignificant by their contemporaries and in the midst of human failure. This, surely, was the lesson of Isaiah in his portrait of Israel itself as God's suffering servant, humiliated, disfigured, seemingly struck by God, suffering not for its own sins but for the sins of others (Isa 52:13–53:12). Could not the very details of the crucifixion of Jesus be found in the picture painted in advance by the psalmist (Psalm 22)? And was not Jesus in his suffering reliving the experience of all those righteous sufferers whose laments rang out in so many psalms, only to be followed by praise of God's anticipated deliverance (e.g., Psalm 69)? They, too, had tasted the treachery of trusted friends (Ps 41:9), and the betrayal of Jesus by Judas had its counterpart in the career of King David himself (2 Sam 17:23; Matt 27:5).

There remained the problem of the continuing unbelief of the chosen people. But was the lack of response to their proclamation of the resurrection any more unusual than the situation that had confronted other prophets in the past? Was it not for precisely this refusal to believe the prophetic message that Isaiah had rebuked his fellow countrymen (Isa 6:9-10; Mark 4:12)?

The Teaching of Jesus

The constant study of the Scriptures was accompanied by instruction on the kingdom of God. The scriptural expertise of trained scribes was coupled with the living memory of men and women who had shared in Jesus' life. Disciples became teachers as they repeated the sayings and parables in which Jesus had taught them the wonder of God's gift and the ways in which to respond to it. They recalled episodes from his life in which he had communicated the message of the kingdom in healings and forgiveness and fellowship with sinners. Gradually teachers built up repertoires of these sayings and stories.

The teachers of the Jesus movement had no need to develop a totally new moral system. In fact it is likely that much of the teaching of Jesus has not been recorded because it was practically the same as that of other Jewish teachers. It was precisely where his attitudes differed from traditional Jewish teaching that it was recalled. When they were asked questions that had been put to Jesus, questions, for example, concerning divorce or paying taxes to Rome, they had ready-made responses in his remembered words. Other points on which he differed from his peers were recalled in stories about his controversies with scribes, Sadducees, and Pharisees.

It is clear that the exact words of Jesus were not regarded as sacrosanct. Even the Our Father, the prayer that served as summary of his prayer and teaching on the kingdom, has been preserved for us in two different versions in the Gospels (Matt 7:9-13; Luke 11:2-4). The phrases he used in the Sermon on the Mount were not constantly repeated verbatim but taken as models and adapted to other situations that arose after his death (Matt 5:11). They no longer lived in the situation of the disciples who had shared Jesus' life; gradually they came to appreciate the immensity of the change that Jesus had brought about through his death and resurrection. The kingdom of God that had been embodied in Jesus during his life had entered a final phase, and the Spirit of God had come on them to complete in this final age the mission it had commenced in the life of Jesus.

The Work of the Prophets

We are much better informed about the work of prophets than of teachers. On several occasions prophets and teachers are bracketed together, but the figure of the prophet stands out much more clearly in the pages of the New Testament. We learn of their activity from its earliest book (1 Thess 5:19-22); and one of its latest, the Apocalypse, is itself a work of Christian prophecy. For the early decades we draw once again on Paul and Luke, though it is from the latter that we hear about the activity of prophets in the church of Jerusalem. Their information can be supplemented by inferences drawn from the sayings source, Q, which is probably the work of a group of Jewish Christian prophets in Palestine.

From Pentecost on, Luke's story is punctuated by cameos of people "filled with the Holy Spirit" (e.g., Acts 4:8; 13:9-11). These include people like the Jerusalem prophet Agabus, who predicts a famine that prompts the Antioch community to send a relief mission to Jerusalem (Acts 11:27-30), and who later prophesies the future imprisonment of Paul in Jerusalem in a symbolic gesture by binding his hands and feet (Acts 21:11). Prophets act as envoys from Jerusalem and speak to encourage and strengthen the community to which they are sent (Acts 15:32). The decision of the Jerusalem council is ascribed to prophetic guidance (Acts 15:28). Prophets from Jerusalem appear in Antioch, Caesarea, Tyre; others, it seems, remain in one place. Some of these prophets are male, others female (Acts 21:9).

All of our sources assume that prophecy is part of the Spirit's normal endowment of a Christian community. This is not to say that every Christian enjoyed the gift of prophecy; prophets were a limited group in the community who exercised a specialized function, usually in the setting of worship. Apostles and teachers were custodians and representatives of the tradition, interpreters of the Scriptures, and of the teaching of Jesus remembered from the sayings of his earthly life. Prophets were like the prophets of Israel in the past, divinely commissioned spokespersons who delivered to the community revelations received directly from God or words of the risen Lord. The community's evangelists and preachers presented a sermon they had prepared; prophets spoke spontaneously and as if under compulsion, not in tongues but in articulate speech. Prophecy was not a skill to be acquired and perfected by practice but an impulse of the Spirit, enabling the prophet here and now to mediate the word of the living, risen Lord to the community, spelling out the demands of discipleship in this place at this time.

Prophets passed judgment on community situations, they encouraged, threatened, and consoled. At times they may simply have repeated known sayings of Jesus; at times they elaborated on them in words that were acknowledged by the believers to whom they were addressed as coming from the risen Lord himself. Scholars commonly hold that a number of these sayings of Christian prophets have been incorporated in the Gospels and are ascribed to Jesus, together with words spoken by him during his earthly life. Thus far they disagree on criteria by which to distinguish them, but it is likely that the sayings of Jesus in the Q source incorporate the prophecies of early Christian prophets together with authentic sayings of Jesus.

7 Community Organization

The Range of Diversity

United though they were in their belief in the risen Jesus as Messiah and in their eager apocalyptic expectation, there was still a wide range of attitudes to be found among the earliest members of the Jesus movement. They were, indeed, all Jews, but as has been said, Judaism at that time embraced many different sects, some of them claiming to be the only authentic Jews, none of them generally acknowledged as alone the "orthodox," or normative, Judaism. Despite Luke's idealized picture of harmonious unity, the Jesus movement was composed from its very beginning of groups of Jews who differed in significant ways, especially in their attitudes to the Law of Moses and the importance of the Temple and its worship.

Luke himself underlines this diversity in the catalogue of the countries of origin of those foreign-born Jews living in Jerusalem who made up part of the audience of the first preachers and from whom the first converts were drawn (Acts 2:8-11). He lists countries from Persia in the east to Libya in the west, from Rome and the provinces of Asia Minor to the Ukraine. It is true that he utilizes a stereotyped catalogue of the nations current at the time to illustrate the universality of the audience, but the earliest community certainly included members such as Barnabas, a Jew from Cyprus (Acts 4:36); Nicholas from Antioch, a Greek convert to Judaism (Acts 6:5); and probably Simon from Cyrene in North Africa (Mark 15:21).

Among Jews born in Palestine there was diversity enough. The core group of disciples, men and women, were from rural Galilee, often regarded as less observant of the finer points of the Law and certainly much further removed from the influence of Temple worship and the control of the religious leaders than urban Jews in Jerusalem. Those who had belonged to different Jewish sects such as disciples of John the Baptist, Essenes, Pharisees, and priests were distinguished by their characteristic approaches to Jewish practices of piety like prayer and fasting and the observance of laws concerning tithes and clean and unclean foods. Different groups followed different calendars in their observance of the Jewish feasts.

Jews born outside Palestine brought with them a range of attitudes that added to this cultural and religious mixture. A Jew born and brought up in Jerusalem was likely to be characterized by an enthusiastic admiration for the Temple and its worship. Many migrants from the Diaspora shared this enthusiasm, though others clearly did not. Essenes attracted to the new movement were strongly opposed to the worship in the Temple and its priestly leaders. Jews born in Palestine may well have been prone to identify all Gentiles with those Gentiles they were most familiar with, the mercenary soldiers in the service of Rome who enforced an oppressive pagan regime. Jews from the Diaspora, from Antioch or North Africa or the great university city of Alexandria, were more likely to have an understanding of the positive values of Hellenistic culture and a sympathetic appreciation of its moral ideals.

Hellenists and Hebrews

Since Luke is at pains to paint a picture of a community one in heart and soul (Acts 2:32), it is not surprising that we find little evidence of this diversity in the Acts of the Apostles. The clearest indication is to be found in the story of the dispute between the two groups called Hellenists and Hebrews. As Luke tells the story it concerns a complaint by a group called the Hellenists about discrimination against the widows in their group in the daily distribution of food to the poor by another group called the Hebrews. The dispute is resolved by the Twelve, who call a community assembly, which agrees unanimously with their decision to devote themselves entirely to preaching and to institute another group of seven members to take charge of this service (Acts 6:1-6).

It is generally understood that the two groups were distinguished by their mother tongue. The Hebrews were Palestinian-born Jews who spoke Aramaic; the Hellenists were foreign-born Jews who spoke Greek. Two details of this apparently simple story alert the reader to Luke's simplification of a more complex underlying issue. All of the seven appointed have Greek names; and though they are chosen to replace the Twelve in the distribution of relief, the only function we find any of them fulfilling in the sequel is the very ministry of the word, which the Twelve claim as their own special task.

Behind Luke's account of harmony restored by innovative apostolic leadership lies the historical reality of two different language groups in the earliest Jerusalem community, each with its own organization, and the ensuing friction in their mutual relations. Since a Jew who spoke only Greek could not share in prayer and the explanation of the Scriptures with a Jew who spoke only Aramaic, these different languages also implied separate worship. Not all synagogue worship in Jerusalem was conducted in Aramaic. There were synagogues in Jerusalem where worship was conducted in Greek and possibly others where other languages were used.

The differences ran much deeper than language. Among the Greek-speaking Jews attracted to the Jesus movement there were some, at least, who were distinguished from other Jews not only by language but by their radical views. These views were represented by Stephen, the leader of the seven, whose preaching in Greek-speaking synagogues aroused the wrath of other more traditional Jews who accused him of speaking against the Law and the Temple and put him to death (Acts 6:9-14).

More traditionally minded members of the Jesus movement may well have been quite as alarmed at the radical views of its Hellenist members as those Jews who instigated the persecution that followed. In their enthusiasm for the Temple some Hebrew members of the Jesus movement were probably more in sympathy with Jews who did not accept Jesus as Messiah than they were with the Hellenists who did. Be that as it may, the existence of these two clearly distinct groups in the Jesus movement in the earliest period in Jerusalem suggests that there were other distinct groups as well. Their members would have occupied different positions across a spectrum of Jewish practice and piety ranging from the very exact observance of the Law, for which James the brother of the Lord was later to become famous, to a practical disregard for Temple and Law, which many Jews who belonged to the Jesus movement judged every bit as scandalous as many Jews who did not.

Once Again . . . Luke's Picture

It may be well to recall at this point that the Acts of the Apostles differs a great deal from the kind of history writing that twentieth-century authors try to provide their readers. Half a century after the events he describes, Luke shows that the religion and way of life that missioners like the Hellenists and then Paul had brought to the Hellenistic world of his readers embodied the same dynamism as did the pentecostal groups in Jerusalem, who in their turn were founded on the original disciples of Jesus.

He does not write as an eyewitness; rather, he draws on the recollections of others–stories told and retold over the intervening half-century about the original heroes of the faith, examples of seeming failure and even persecution that had ultimately led to the spread of the gospel from Jerusalem to their own distant Hellenistic world. His picture is one of a tightly knit group under the leadership of Peter acting in unison with the twelve apostles. The apostles proclaim the message of the resurrection. The whole community is united in prayer at the Temple and in their homes and devoted to the teaching of the apostles. The leaders are assisted by presbyters and relief workers in their care of the poor.

Our discussion so far suggests that the historical reality of the Jesus movement in its Jerusalem origins was much less homogeneous and orderly. It would seem better to envision it as a number of distinct groups of Jews gathered around different leaders. Some of these were disciples of Jesus, men and women who had been disciples of Jesus, had suffered the shock of his death, and had witnessed the risen Jesus either in Galilee or in Jerusalem. Others were charismatic leaders from Palestine or the Diaspora who may never have known Jesus but had been convinced by the testimony of those disciples. They brought a different mentality and a different kind of piety to the mission, which they undertook with equal enthusiasm.

Koinonia

Growth brought its own problems. Members of the Jesus movement who lived in Jerusalem could earn their living by working at their trade or as day laborers. Some were supported by the extended family to which they belonged. For many others, people from Galilee or the lands of the Diaspora separated from the usual support systems of home, family, and occupation, joining this new group in Jerusalem meant relying entirely on the support of others.

Luke writes about what he calls "koinonia," a lifestyle based on an ideal of sharing. He describes the Jerusalem community as a group where possessions are held in common (Acts 4:32). The Essenes at Qumran were such a group, placing all their possessions at the service of the community. One of their names was "the one-ness," or "the community," and Luke's Greek term may be his version of the same name.

Apart from these Palestinian connections, the term koinonia also evokes some of the great ideals and dreams of the Hellenistic world of Luke's readers. The dream of a world in which private property was unknown was as old as Plato. Maxims of the philosopher Pythagoras about friends being equals and one soul and about the possessions of friends being common property had been bandied about for centuries. There were groups in the Hellenistic world, too, like the disciples of Pythagoras, whose community life was an attempt to live up to those ideals.

The first Jerusalem community, as Luke presents it, is the fulfillment of that Hellenistic ideal. This koinonia creates an environment where God's promises for the final age are already fulfilled because poverty is abolished (Acts 4:34; cf. Deut 15:4). Their sharing of material possessions is the expression of a much deeper sharing, that of their faith. It is this that makes them "one heart and one soul"; they are not simply friends but "the community of those who believed" (Acts 4:32).

It is an idealized picture. Luke has presented as a norm the kind of generosity shown by some individual members, people like Barnabas, remembered for his selling his belongings to share with others (Acts 4:36f.). Where the Essenes bound themselves to give their entire earnings into the hands of their supervisor for the support of the community, the members of the Jesus movement were under no such obligation. Their ideal of putting an end to need was only imperfectly attained; twenty years later the Jerusalem community remained a poor people, and Paul pledged his Gentile churches to support the poor in Jerusalem as a token of the faith and spiritual riches they shared.

Leadership

As the example of the Essenes shows, even an apocalyptic sect living in intense expectation of a final age, which it believes to be imminent, cannot survive without leadership and organization. The Essene community was preparing for an imminent battle against the powers of darkness and the end of this world, but their community rule shows that their lifestyle was strictly organized. Rank in the community was clearly defined and determined the order in which people took their place at table. There was a clear division between priests and laypeople. The community was divided symbolically into twelve tribes and organized into small groups of about ten people, each of which had its own supervisor who was entrusted with pastoral care of the group as well as discipline and financial administration, and its own priest to lead in worship. These small groups met from time to time in general assembly and were governed by a supreme council of twelve men as leaders of the twelve tribes, and three priests.

We have already noted some of the similarities between the Essenes and the Jesus movement. Luke's story suggests the calling of a general assembly for important matters (Acts 6:2, 5; 15:12) and highlights the leadership role of the Twelve. But the extent of diversity within the groups that constituted the Jesus movement meant that its pattern of organization could not follow the tightly organized system of Qumran. It is impossible to reconstruct that pattern in detail, because though Luke and Paul point clearly to details that concerned them, they leave us totally uninformed about others that interest us. Luke, moreover, is to a great extent simply stamping the pattern of church life he wants to inculcate in the Hellenistic communities of his time on the image of the community of their origins in Jerusalem.

Peter, the Twelve, and the Apostles

Peter is the person who emerges most clearly as leader in the earliest period. He dominates the early pages of Acts. His name heads the list of the Eleven (Acts 1:13); he initiates the process for the replacement of Judas (Acts 1:20); he is preacher and spokesman for the community (Acts 2:14-36; 4:8-12). He is charismatic healer (Acts 3:1-10) and the subject of special divine protection (Acts 5:17-21). We can question the extent to which Luke has idealized this portrait, but the prominence attributed to Peter by Luke is also attested by Paul in his various visits to Jerusalem and in his well-known disagreement with Peter in Antioch. He places Peter first among witnesses of the risen Jesus (1 Cor 15:5) and recognizes him as missionary apostle to the Jews as well as spokesman for the Twelve (Gal 1:18; 2:8f.).

Together with Peter and at the heart of the core group stand the Twelve. Some have denied the historical existence of the Twelve and seen them as part of a symbolic picture painted by the later Church. We have seen, however, that the pattern of leadership by a group of twelve already existed in Judaism in the Essene community. Inside Judaism this was a natural way for a body claiming to be the authentic Israel to organize. Paul confirms the existence of the Twelve and includes them among those who had been privileged by an appearance of the risen Jesus (1 Cor 15:5). They were chosen by Jesus during his lifetime and established by him as the twelve patriarchs of the renewed people of God that his mission was intended to bring about (Matt 19:28).

Apart from Jesus' betrayer, Judas, only the two sets of brothers, Peter and Andrew, James and John, appear as disciples who were remembered as individuals in the early Church. In the Acts the Twelve, simply identified as "the apostles," appear regularly with Peter in Jerusalem, proclaiming in unison with him the message of the resurrection (Acts 2:37; 5:29), but there is little evidence of any missionary activity on their part outside Jerusalem and no evidence that any of them were ever leaders of a local church. By the time Luke wrote, most of them were dead, Peter and Paul for twenty years. Even though the Twelve *as a group* were securely lodged in the community memory, no trace of their individual careers remained except for John, who is regularly associated with Peter (Acts 3:1; 8:14; Gal 2:9), and his brother James (Acts 12:2). By the time this James was put to death by Herod Agrippa in 43 C.E. Peter had disappeared from the Jerusalem scene.

The gospel writers Matthew, Mark, and especially Luke refer to the Twelve as "apostles" (Mark 6:30; Matt 10:2; Luke 6:13). One might be led to think that the Twelve were the only persons in the early Church who had a claim to that title. It is clear, however, that the title "apostle" applied in the earliest decades to others than the Twelve. We shall explore in later pages the meaning of the term "apostle" and the range of persons and activities to which it applies. For the moment we note that when the Twelve are described as "apostles," the evangelists are using the language not of Jesus himself but of the early Church. By reserving the title to the Twelve, companions of Jesus during his life and witnesses of his resurrection, Luke made them stand out as guarantors of the tradition inaugurated by Jesus and handed down to his own generation. The price he paid in asserting continuity in this way was to paint all other "apostles" right out of his picture of the early Church.

The Women Disciples

Luke's tableau of the nucleus community awaiting in the upper room the coming of the Spirit at Pentecost includes "the women, Mary the mother of Jesus and his brothers" (Acts 1:14). The women he refers to are the ones who "had followed him in Galilee and ministered to him." Mark first mentions them on Calvary (Mark 15:40), but Luke introduces them much earlier in his story, in which they follow Jesus from Galilee (Luke 8:1-3). Members of this group accompanied the body of Jesus to the tomb, and it was they who discovered the tomb empty and announced the message of the resurrection to the disciples (Luke 24:1-10). Apart from Luke's anonymous if honorable mention in the group in Jerusalem awaiting the coming of the Spirit, they then disappear without trace from the pages of the New Testament.

What is most striking is the disappearance of Mary Magdalene, who is always named first in the group of women disciples on Calvary and at the tomb. Either in company with other women (Matt 28:8-10) or on her own (John 1:10-18), she is first to "see the Lord" and proclaim the good news to the disciples. In our New Testament sources Mary Magdalene joins the other women disciples in oblivion after the resurrection, while the male disciples, initially discredited by their desertion during the passion, return to the scene totally rehabilitated as leaders of the Jerusalem community.

It is impossible to imagine that the message of the women disciples was limited to their brother disciples. They surely took an active part in the proclamation to the Jews, both in Jerusalem and in Galilee. It may well have been that in formal legal processes the witness of a woman was not admitted in Jewish practice, but it is only reasonable to judge that the testimony of those women and their claim to be witnesses of the risen Jesus would have carried conviction generally, but particularly among devout Jewish women.

James and "The Brothers of the Lord"

The leader of the Jerusalem church in later years was James, "brother of the Lord" (Gal 1:19). Many scholars interpret the term "brother" in what they claim is its most natural sense, as "blood brother," making James a son of Joseph and Mary. Catholics, influenced in their interpretation by the longstanding tradition of Mary's perpetual virginity, take it to mean "close relation, kinsman," and speculate on the degree of the blood relationship between James and Jesus. Some suggest "foster brother," others simply the generic "cousin."

The group referred to in the Gospels as "brothers of the Lord" (Mark 6:3) did not follow him during his ministry. Mark, in fact, depicts his whole family as misunderstanding him (Mark 3:21) and explains that it is the disciples who are "brother and sister and mother" to him (Mark 3:35). Though James was not a follower of Jesus during his life, Paul lists him among those to whom the risen Jesus appeared (1 Cor 15:7) and, presumably on this basis, calls him an "apostle" (Gal 1:19). He places him alongside Peter and John at his meeting in Jerusalem, one who shares their status as "columns" of the Jerusalem community (Gal 2:9). James was invoked as an authority as far away as Galatia and in Corinth, and missioners claiming his authority were among Paul's opponents. He was the leader of the Jewish Christian community in Jerusalem when Paul led his Gentile Christians there on pilgrimage with their gift of money in 58 C.E. (Acts 21:18). Well known as an observant Jew, he was put to death by the high priest Ananias shortly before the destruction of Jerusalem in 70 C.E.

What were the respective spheres of influence of Peter and the Twelve and James? It is impossible to reconstruct a detailed picture of the exercise of authority in the earliest period. Even Luke, who highlights the leadership role of Peter, has no qualms in writing that "the apostles in Jerusalem sent Peter and John" to Samaria (Acts 8:14), as if the leader appointed by Jesus himself was still subject to a collegial decision. In the course of time different groups would develop their own styles of leadership. In the beginning Jewish believers accepted the leadership of those who had been the closest associates of Jesus during his life. The case of James, the devout Jewish kinsman of Jesus who became a believer only after the resurrection, suggests that other Jewish believers were attracted by factors as reassuring and as natural as the mixture of Jewish piety and family relationship that James represented.

Suggested Reading

General Reference

Achetemeier, P., ed. *Harper's Bible Dictionary*. San Francisco: Harper and Row, 1985. A handy one-volume reference to topics, persons, places.

Brown, Raymond E., J. A. Fitzmyer, and R. Murphy, eds. *The New Jerome Biblical Commentary*. Englewood Cliffs, N.J.: Prentice Hall, 1990. The most useful one-volume reference book. Especially useful are its historical surveys and topical articles on Jesus, Paul, early Church.

Freedman, D. N., ed. *The Anchor Bible Dictionary*. New York: Doubleday, 1992. A massive six-volume compendium dealing in scholarly depth with individual topics. It shows the current state of scholarly opinion and debate on areas of scriptural research of many kinds.

Freyne, S. A. *The World of the New Testament*. Wilmington, Del.: Michael Glazier, 1980. A simple overview of the Greek and Roman worlds, the Jewish religion, and the origins of Christianity.

Newsom, C. A., and S. H. Ringe, eds. *The Women's Bible Commentary*. London: S.P.C.K., 1992. Summarizes the contributions of feminist scholars to the analysis of each book of the Bible.

Winter, B. W., ed. *The Book of Acts in Its First-Century Setting*. Grand Rapids: Eerdmans. A six-volume series commenced in 1993 with contributions from experts in the field of history, literary criticism, and theological interpretation.

Particular Areas

(The following easily accessible books will help the reader to pursue some of the areas summarized in the text.)

Brown, R. E., K. P. Donfried, and J. Reumann, eds. *Peter in the New Testament.* Minneapolis: Augsburg Publishing House; New York: Paulist Press, 1973. A collaborative assessment.

Dunn, J. G. D. *Jesus' Call to Discipleship.* Cambridge University Press, 1992.

Elliott, John H. *What Is Social-Science Criticism?* Minneapolis: Fortress Press, 1993.

Fitzmyer, J. A. *A Christological Catechism: New Testament Answers.* 2d ed. New York: Paulist Press, 1991.

_____. *Responses to 101 Questions on the Dead Sea Scrolls.* New York: Paulist Press, 1992.

Kee, H. C. *What Can We Know About Jesus?* Cambridge University Press, 1990.

McKenzie, S. L. and S. R. Hynes, eds. *To Each Its Own Meaning: An Introduction to Biblical Criticisms and Their Application.* Louisville: Westminster/John Knox, 1993.

Neyrey, J. *The Resurrection Stories.* Wilmington, Del.: Michael Glazier, 1988.

Osiek, C. *What Are They Saying About the Social Setting of the New Testament?* New York: Paulist Press, 2d ed., 1992.

Perkins, P. *Jesus as Teacher.* Cambridge University Press, 1990.

Powell, M. A. *What Are They Saying About Acts?* New York: Paulist Press, 1991.

Riches, J. *The World of Jesus: First Century Judaism in Crisis.* Cambridge University Press, 1990.

Theissen, G. *The Shadow of the Galilean: The Quest of the Historical Jesus in Narrative Form.* London: SCM Press, 1987.

Part 2

Antioch

8 Antioch

The Hellenistic World

When the first Christian missioners arrived in Antioch they entered a typical Greco-Roman city, a center of Hellenistic culture. The adjective "Hellenistic" simply means "Greek." Though it could as well apply to the way of life of the Greek city-states of antiquity, it is commonly reserved to the era that began in the years between 336 and 323 B.C.E., when Alexander the Great created a world empire stretching from Athens to the Indian frontier. The centuries that followed were characterized by the spread of Greek culture by his successors throughout the immense territory he subdued. The Roman general Octavian rang down the curtain on the Hellenistic age when he defeated Mark Antony in the battle of Actium and was acknowledged as the Emperor Caesar Augustus by the Roman senate in 27 B.C.E., but by that time Hellenistic culture had captivated the Roman conquerors themselves.

Not only was Alexander an unparalleled military commander capable of conquering a vast empire, he was also a visionary leader driven by an impelling ideal. He dreamed of Greek culture as the unifying force that would forge a cultural as well as political unity through his domains and make of them truly one world. As a teenager he had been tutored by no less a master of Greek thought than the philosopher Aristotle; with Alexander and his armies classical Greek culture began to permeate a world empire.

He founded many cities (the ancient historian Plutarch numbered no less than seventy) at important strategic and commercial points in his empire, all of which were instruments of this policy. They were modeled on the traditional Greek *polis,* or city-state, a small self-supporting community with its own territory centered on one town and governed by a democratically elected council and officials responsible to the assembly of the citizens. The cities founded by Alexander and his successors enjoyed a much more limited independence as parts of an empire or kingdom, but they remained enclaves of Greek culture, which was the basis of their government and their institutions.

Hellenistic cities were united by a common language. The founding colonists were usually Greek soldiers retiring from the army, who were encouraged by land grants or other concessions to settle and marry locally, and merchants attracted from older Greek cities. Outlying areas might retain their mother tongue; inside the town, at least, Greek replaced the local language. Greek methods of education imparted a knowledge of Greek literature, philosophy and science. In sculpture and painting, pottery and glassware, household furniture and decoration, Greek styles dictated local fashion. Greek customs and styles in dress prevailed; so did Greek sports and athletic contests. The end result of this encounter of the local cultures with the Greek way of life was a cultural environment common to these cities in which Greek manners submerged local ways; though the Greek settlers, despite their easy assumption of cultural superiority, were not immune to the attractions of some of the local customs and especially to the appeal of Oriental religions.

From the Seleucids to the Romans

Antioch was established in 300 B.C.E. by Seleucus, the man who gave his name to the Seleucid dynasty, which controlled much of the territory of Alexander's empire for the next two hundred and fifty years. He named the city after his father Antiochus, one of Alexander's generals. Seleucus himself had commenced his career as an officer in Alexander's army; and when Alexander's empire was divided among his successors in 323 B.C.E., Seleucus gained control of much of Asia Minor and Mesopotamia, until his territory extended as far as India. He established his eastern capital at Seleucia on the Tigris, but after a decisive battle in 301, he secured his access to the Mediterranean and gained control of Syria. He founded Antioch as his capital in the west.

For the next century control of Syria and Palestine was contested between the Seleucids in the north and the rival dynasty in the south, the Ptolemies in Egypt. Despite a number of defeats suffered by successive Seleucid kings, control of Palestine was finally wrested from the Ptolemies by the Seleucid king Antiochus the Great in 198 B.C.E. By the turn of the second century B.C.E., however, Rome had begun its westward march, and Seleucid power was on the wane. In 190 Antiochus lost his kingdom in Asia Minor when the Romans routed his fleet and army. By 143 the successful Maccabean revolution had resulted in an independent Jewish state in Palestine, and in its last sixty years the Seleucid dynasty was weakened by internal rivalry with two different branches contesting the throne.

The Romans arrived in Antioch in 64 B.C.E. Pompey conquered Syria, which became a Roman province governed by a proconsul sent by the senate. Antioch retained its prominence as a center of communication between Palestine and Asia Minor and the major staging area for Roman operations against the Persians in Mesopotamia. By the first century Syria's military importance was such that it was placed under the direct control of the Roman emperor, exercised through a legate, and Antioch was ranked as the third most important city in the empire after Rome and Alexandria.

The Hellenistic City

Hellenistic cities were usually laid out on a pattern similar to that of the *polis* of the classical age. As the political and commercial center of city life, the *agora,* or marketplace, occupied pride of place, surrounded on three sides by its *stoa,* a series of roofed colonnades that provided shelter in all weathers. The main public buildings were the council chamber, the gymnasium, the theater, and the stadium. The gymnasium was devoted to education, both physical and intellectual; it was equipped with a *palaestra,* an open-air exercise court covered in sand with school rooms and changing rooms. The theater was devoted to drama, oratory, and citizens' assemblies. The stadium was the venue for the regular athletic contests that were an important part of the celebration of feasts. There were many sanctuaries of different kinds, enclosed areas with statues, springs, shrines and inscriptions and temples to the range of divinities worshiped locally.

The city depended on the produce of the surrounding villages and countryside for its survival. Most of the land belonged to wealthy landholders who owned country villas on their farms and well-appointed houses in the city and who let their property out to tenants. Small parcels of land were held by peasant landholders and farmed by themselves and their family or sharecroppers, but harsh taxation gradually concentrated ownership in fewer and fewer hands. Peasants were always engaged in subsistence farming at best; one bad season or military requisition of crops could trigger the spiral of debt that ended in selling themselves or their families into slavery.

On the other hand, the campaigns of Alexander had opened up new trade routes and made the new cities centers of commerce and industry where merchants could trade in minerals, foodstuffs, textiles, and luxury goods and where artisans could ply their trades. New fortunes were made, a new middle class developed, and of course, a new, elaborate network of taxation officials came into existence. New religions accompanied this developing traffic; Roman officials carried their religions to foreign postings and brought Oriental religions back to Rome with them; new settlers from foreign lands sought out the company of fellow countrymen to worship the gods of their homeland.

Life in the City

Measured by modern standards, these were not large cities. Athens in its golden age probably numbered no more than 200,000 inhabitants. At its foundation Antioch was no more than a square mile in area and at its greatest extent its walls enclosed no more than twice that space, much of which was taken up by public buildings and monuments. The vast majority of the population lived in tiny cubicles in multi-storied tenements, unheated and poorly ventilated, as crowded as any modern industrial slum and even more vulnerable to infectious diseases. Scholars calculate that the average population density of those cities was higher than that of the most crowded areas of New York or Bombay. The splendor of the public buildings and the large public spaces was scant compensation for the lack of privacy that obliged most people to spend much of their life on the street. Problems of sanitation, garbage disposal, and water supply contributed to poor health, recurrent epidemics, and high mortality rates so that half the children died at birth or during infancy. The mixture of many ethnic groups living at such close quarters led to regular racial friction and the outbreak of riots.

Not all the inhabitants shared equally in the benefits of city life. Citizenship with its right to a role in government was confined to an elite group. Nearly one third of the population consisted of slaves, many of whom had been deported from their homeland in the wake of ruinous wars with no hope of improving their position. In a search for support to offset the depersonalization of that world people had recourse to voluntary associations, clubs, and societies of many kinds, some purely social, some for worship, some just to assure their members the dignity of a proper burial. Sometimes as few as a dozen, or twenty, rarely more than a hundred people banded together, chose a name, drew up a constitution and elected officers who often bore quite grandiose titles. Some drew their adherents from a given household, others from a group of similar ethnic origin, perhaps Syrian or Egyptian, to worship the gods of their homeland. Since a major difficulty for a large group was to find a meeting place, the patron who provided it occupied a position of special honor.

Another of the institutions of the Hellenistic city that was to occupy an important place in developing Christianity was the extended household. This basic political and economic unit consisted of the whole group connected with a given "house." It included the father with his wife, sons and daughters, dependent relatives, servants, attendants, and slaves. Though the head of the house exercised total legal control over its members, each of them found security and a sense of belonging in their individual functions and mutual responsibility. In this urban environment the household took the place of family and clan in the villages of Palestine, providing security and a sense of solidarity but also imposing its standards and a different set of customs.

The traditional role of married women in this world was the management of the household, though, at least in the eastern section of the Roman Empire noblewomen could move about freely in public. The example of Lydia (Acts 16:14) shows that women were engaged in commerce and manufacture, indeed, of luxury goods. There are inscriptions of the Hellenistic era that show that some women achieved public prominence as benefactors and officials of cities. They are named as members of various clubs and officers in voluntary associations, sometimes as sponsors or patrons who offered the use of their home as a venue or provided for some of the association's expenses. The new religions, too, seem to have offered opportunities for women to lead in worship, to act as priestess or leader in private family worship.

Religion in the Hellenistic World

The Hellenistic era brought about great changes in the way people saw their world and, hence, in their religious feeling. The official religion of ancient Greece consisted essentially of a series of public rites and ceremonies to secure the favor of the gods. The gods thus honored, such as the sovereign god, Zeus, his consort, Hera, sons like Apollo and Dionysus and daughters like Athena and Aphrodite were those of the Olympian pantheon, whose deeds and relationships were chronicled by Homer and the classical poets. They were, in effect, guarantors of law and order in the society and personifications of the virtues of the citizen. This kind of religion was a civic duty; sacrifices, votive offerings, prayer formulas were the necessary machinery to secure the assistance of the powers on whom the *polis* depended for its security and survival.

This official religion left unsatisfied the daily needs of individuals such as health, domestic harmony, material prosperity. These were met by recourse to more approachable gods and spirits in the many local sanctuaries, sacred springs, grottoes and woods, or to less remote and more accessible Olympian gods like Asclepius, son of Apollo, a god of pity and compassion, whose many sanctuaries were thronged with people seeking healing from all kinds of maladies. Deeper needs like assurance in the face of death or the yearning for personal communion with the gods were satisfied through mystery religions such as those of Eleusis, which involved initiation into a community claiming, through ritual enactment of a myth, to enter into communion with the god whose relations with human beings it depicted.

With the coming of the world empire of Alexander and the continuing encounter of Greek religion with the religions of the east in the cosmopolitan Hellenistic cities, human horizons were vastly extended. The stature of local divinities shrank in comparison with the gods of Syria, Asia, and Egypt, whose worship spread throughout the Hellenistic world and satisfied personal needs that official worship could not touch. The events of their own history revealed the immense forces at work in the making of empires and kingdoms, the overpowering might of armies at the control of kings. Because he embodied that awesome power, the king or emperor was regarded as a divine being who guaranteed the happiness of his subjects and the prosperity of the realm.

While official religion in the Hellenistic world became more splendid and formal, the uncertainties of life in the Hellenistic city heightened the sense of need and anxiety experienced by people of every culture confronted with the mysteries of life and death. The ever-present possibility of famine, disease, and slavery and the sense of rootlessness and social dislocation heightened the feeling that life was in the power of an uncontrollable, unpredictable, blind chance or fate with an impersonal divine power governing the destinies of individuals and society. The future of the city as well as that of individuals lay not in their own hands but depended on their *tyche,* or fortune, a force capricious and beyond human reach.

Magicians attempted to find the proper spells or incantations that would bind those mysterious, hostile forces that peopled the earth and the air. Astrologers studied the movement of the stars to predict their influence on human affairs. The most popular way, however, in which people sought to escape the influence of adverse powers and to enter into communion with a god who cared for the individual well-being of its adherents, especially after death, was through the mystery religions, which had come into their own in the Hellenistic era. The most popular of the foreign gods at the beginning of the first century was the Egyptian goddess Isis, a woman and a mother whose maternal care, more powerful than fate, extended to all humankind. In secret rites of initiation, through sacred meals and other rituals, people sought access to a life that would free them from social alienation and the fear of death.

Official Roman religion was quite as formal as that of the Greeks, a round of ceremonies whose objective was to promote the welfare of the state. Ordinary people looked rather to the divine patrons and protectors of family life and prosperity, the lesser gods of hearth and home. Since the greatest and seemingly irresistible force observable in world events was the power of the empire itself, divine homage was paid to Rome and temples were dedicated in honor of the empire. If ever there was a human embodiment of divine power it was surely the Roman emperor; little wonder, then, if some emperors demanded to be honored as divine beings in ceremonies that included a prayer for the welfare of Rome, Caesar, and the empire.

Antioch

Our knowledge of Antioch and its history is derived from ancient authors and modern archaeologists. Written material concerning Antioch from the Seleucid era itself is sparse; it becomes more frequent in Roman times and abundant in later Christian centuries. Earthquakes and centuries of erosion caused by water coursing down the steep slopes of Mount Silpius have covered the remains of the Hellenistic city to a depth of ten meters. Annual excavations were conducted at Antakya in modern Turkey under the auspices of Princeton University from 1932 to 1939. Parts of the early city walls, a hippodrome, sections of aqueducts, and an ancient bridge over the Orontes can still be seen.

Seleucus first built a naval base in one of the finest harbors in the eastern Mediterranean. This port, close to the mouth of the river Orontes, became a major fortified city, protected to the north by Mount Pierius, which rises to four thousand feet above sea level and whose fortifications were virtually impregnable. It equaled Ephesus in importance as a major naval base of the Seleucid Empire. The emperor regarded it as one of the most important of the many cities he founded; he endowed it with his own name, Seleucia Pieria, and it served as his capital for most of his reign.

Seleucus next built the city of Antioch to secure control of the land routes. It was less than a day's walk inland from the port, located at a bend in the Orontes where the river breaks out of the Syrian rift valley on the final stage of its passage to the Mediterranean. The city was laid out as a square between the left bank of the river and the slopes of Mount Silpius on the east. The river valley and the plain to the north, together with its lake, guaranteed a regular supply of grain, olives, grapes, fish, and a variety of garden vegetables. Springs in a famous grove sacred to Daphne five miles to the south provided much of the city's water supply, and its long, dry summer made it a very agreeable place to stay.

Connected to the port by the Orontes, the city was a center of communications by land as well as by sea. To the west the highway led through Cilicia across Asia Minor. To the east the commercial and military route led through Aleppo to Mesopotamia and was the natural highway from the interior to the Mediterranean. To the south the road led to the granaries of Syria and Palestine; to the northeast there was access to the high valleys of the upper Euphrates.

Seleucus divided his city into two sections, one for native Syrians and the other for his veterans and followers. Successors of Seleucus extended the city he built. His son Antiochus I, built a walled quarter to the east. Later Seleucid emperors constructed other sections, one on an island in the river connected with its banks by a series of bridges. The luxurious constructions of Antiochus IV had already made of it one of the foremost cities of antiquity when a final section was added late in the second century.

The Romans in their turn contributed to its expansion and decoration. Julius Caesar added a series of public buildings, temples, baths, aqueduct, a new theater, and an amphitheater. Tiberius was honored for his benefactions with a bronze statue erected in a public square dominating the wide colonnaded main road, which had been paved in marble as a gift from Herod the Great. The citizens of Antioch had long been enthusiastic followers of horse racing in the hippodrome; to Roman times can be assigned the beginnings of the Olympic games, which became in time one of the most famous festivals of the Roman world.

At the foundation of Antioch Seleucus satisfied the demands of the official religion by sacrifices to Zeus, who gradually absorbed the functions of various local gods and was acclaimed with many titles. He also installed a statue of Tyche, the good fortune of Antioch, in the form of a robed goddess seated on a rock representing Mount Silpius, wearing a turreted crown representing the walls and gates of the city with a youth at her feet representing the river Orontes. This statue dominated the city and was to stand for a long time. Apollo was honored in a temple at Daphne; other temples were dedicated to Ares, god of war, and Dionysus; while the mystery religions were represented by temples of Isis and Demeter. Archaeologists have uncovered evidence of other temples to gods such as Aphrodite, Artemis, Athena, and Hermes as well as statues of a dozen more. The Romans, in their turn, added temples to their gods and statues of their emperors.

9 From Synagogue to Agora

The Jews in the Diaspora

From the time of the Babylonian Exile in the sixth century there had been Jews living outside Palestine in what came to be known as the Diaspora, or dispersion. In the centuries that followed the Exile either forced deportation in the aftermath of war or voluntary emigration had scattered Jews to the four winds, until they were established in every major city around the eastern Mediterranean. They were to be found not only in Babylon and other parts of Mesopotamia but in Alexandria and the cities of Egypt and as far west as Morocco. They were particularly numerous in Syria because it was so close to Palestine. By the first century of our era there were far more Jews living outside Palestine than inside it. It has been calculated that Jews made up some 10 to 15 percent of the population of the cities of the Roman Empire, a figure of five to six million against a total Palestinian population of perhaps one million.

Some of these Jews had achieved the status of citizens of their city or even of the Roman Empire, but the civic status of most of them was that of resident aliens. As a group the Jews in a city usually constituted what was known in legal terms as a *politeuma*, a semi-autonomous body of residents who, though not citizens, shared certain specified citizen rights. Though Jews living in the Diaspora were never compelled to live in ghettos, a Jewish quarter could be found in practically every Hellenistic city.

Hellenistic rulers generally conceded to these Jewish groups the right to live according to their ancestral laws. They were subject in most things to the law of the land, but they enjoyed considerable internal autonomy in their community affairs, which were conducted according to Jewish law. They were free to maintain their own synagogues and courts, to appoint their officials, and to conduct their own education system. In later centuries under Roman rule these rights were confirmed and the legal status of Jews remained unchanged; in particular they were not obliged to worship Roman gods, and special arrangements permitted them to celebrate imperial festivals without compromising their faith by participating in the ceremonies of emperor worship. Prayers in the synagogues and the Temple were substituted for the ritual gestures of sacrifice to the emperor.

The largest Jewish community in the Diaspora was that of Alexandria. Within a short time from its foundation by Alexander the Great in 331 B.C.E. this city had become the uncontested commercial and cultural center of the Hellenistic world. There were Jews in Alexandria from the time of its foundation; they were duly established as a *politeuma.* Ptolemies and then Romans encouraged them to live according to their ancestral customs. On the eve of the Christian era there were perhaps a million Jews in Egypt, of whom hundreds of thousands lived in Alexandria, which thus occupied a role in the Judaism of that time comparable to that of New York in contemporary Judaism.

However far away they lived, Diaspora Jews looked to Jerusalem as their spiritual center. Jews everywhere looked forward to visiting Jerusalem at least once in their lifetime. In fact, distance often served to idealize their image of the Holy City, so that many who lived at a distance were more attached to it than those who lived there. Officials from Jerusalem made regular visits to Jewish centers in the Diaspora to strengthen the bonds that united Jews throughout the world as one people. Every adult male Jew was obliged to pay an annual tax of a half-shekel to support the Temple, a privilege permitted and indeed defended by the Romans.

Judaism Confronts the Hellenistic World

The Hellenistic environment had an inevitable effect on the attitudes of Diaspora Jews. It was impossible to live in that world, to speak the Greek language, to engage in commercial, civic, and social relations, without undergoing significant change. In Palestine Jews were a subject people; despite their numerical superiority they were constantly reminded of their domination by a pagan power. In many parts of the Diaspora they saw and felt themselves much more as peers and equals of the pagan inhabitants; inscriptions from Miletus in Asia Minor, for example, designate the seats in the theater reserved for Jews. Some Jews were completely assimilated into the Hellenistic way of life; they adopted Greek names, their sons were educated in the gymnasium, and their Jewish faith and identity was attenuated and even dissolved into virtually total conformity with the surrounding pagan culture. The very survival of Judaism over centuries in the Hellenistic world, however, is sufficient testimony to the fidelity of thousands of other Jews and their obstinate adherence to their law and traditions despite the constant pressure of the environment.

Many Jews who clung tenaciously to the faith of their forebears still found much to admire in the Hellenistic way of life, its literature, and philosophy. Judaism not only learned to adapt its message to the needs of the Hellenistic world, it profited by the riches this world offered. In the Greek language it found a more supple means of communication than Aramaic or Hebrew; the images of Greek poets and concepts of Greek philosophers were pressed into service to explain and defend the Jewish faith. How they went about this task can be seen in the Jewish writings in Greek that originated in Alexandria and Egypt at this time. Unfortunately none have come down to us, though many are preserved in fragmentary form in the works of later writers, some of whom were Christians.

The earliest Jewish writer in Greek known to us by name is Demetrius, who wrote a chronicle of Jewish history in Egypt in the third century B.C.E. In the middle of the following century Ezekiel the tragedian employed the forms and rhythms of Greek drama to present the story of the Exodus. At the same time in Alexandria the biblical commentator Aristobulus was using the current Greek literary techniques to produce an allegorical interpretation of the biblical laws, which pagan Alexandrians found offensive, to show that Plato and Pythagoras were familiar with the Law of Moses. Before 50 B.C.E Artapanas in Alexandria was writing his historical romance about Abraham, Joseph, and Moses to clarify misconceptions of the pagans about Judaism. Jewish historical and philosophical works of this period inculcated common themes–monotheism and the evils of idolatry, the way the true God was revealed, and the special position of Israel in God's work of salvation. They developed the arguments and patterns of apologetic, which their Christian successors would exploit when in their turn they addressed the pagans.

A number of these books were eventually incorporated into the Greek Bible. The book of Sirach, or Ecclesiasticus, is a Greek translation made in Egypt in 132 B.C.E of a book composed sixty years earlier and is comparable to Jewish Wisdom literature. The two books of Maccabees tell the story of the Jewish struggle for independence against the Seleucid kings. The first, written originally in Hebrew, is known to us only in a Greek translation; the second, an original Greek composition, is a summary of an earlier work by an African Jew written for the Jews of Alexandria; both are compositions of the late second or early first century B.C.E. The last-written book in the Greek Bible is the Wisdom of Solomon, written in Greek around 50 B.C.E. to strengthen the faith of Jews attracted by the cultural life of Alexandria.

The most celebrated of these Hellenistic Jewish writers was the Alexandrian Philo (ca. 20 B.C.E.–50 C.E.). He was a strict observer of the Law, nourished by the Scriptures, which he accepted as source of all true knowledge, and was at the same time a lover of Greek theater, a keen spectator of the boxing matches in the stadium and the horse races in the hippodrome, and an admirer of Greek poetry and philosophy. His many writings include biblical commentaries as well as philosophical, historical, and apologetic works. In his commentaries on the Scriptures he employed the literary methods of Greek scholars to develop an allegorical explanation of the Scriptures, which enabled him to discover much of Greek philosophy, especially that of Plato, in the pages of the Scriptures. For Philo the wisdom of the great Greek philosophers is a reflection of that of the Jewish Scriptures; Plato, all unknowing, is a disciple of Moses.

The greatest monument to this literary activity of the Jews in the Diaspora is the Greek translation of the Hebrew Scriptures known as the Septuagint, completed in Alexandria in the second century B.C.E. after more than a century of collective effort. Jews in the Diaspora who no longer understood the Hebrew text or spoke the Aramaic language in which it had been explained in the past now had the Scriptures available in the vernacular for use in worship. The Semitic notions and usages of the Hebrew texts were transposed into the familiar terms and concepts of Greek philosophy, so that they could invite their pagan contemporaries to compare this Jewish wisdom with that of their Greek philosophers and suggest that whatever was best in the latter could be found as well in the Jewish Scriptures.

Pagans were attracted to Judaism for many reasons. Intellectuals were attracted by its belief in one God because of their dissatisfaction with the worldview represented by the many gods of the classical pantheon. The simple moral code of Judaism, which was clear and easily understood by all, embodied much of the moral ideal of the Hellenistic philosophers. There was, moreover, a fascination about the mysterious elements of Jewish worship and the strange items of its dietary laws. The observance of the Sabbath and the stability of Jewish family life were other potent factors.

Pagan converts to Judaism were known as "proselytes." They were initiated by the rite of circumcision, sometimes accompanied by the ritual purification of baptism and the presentation of an offering to the Temple, though it is unknown how widespread these latter requirements were in the Diaspora. Other pagans who were attracted by the moral code of Judaism and its monotheistic worship still found themselves unable for a number of reasons to submit to circumcision and observe the dietary laws. They remained closely attached to the synagogue and were known as "god-fearers," or devout people. In some places proselytes and god-fearers were numerous; it is likely that in some synagogues there were as many and even more of them than there were Jews.

Beginnings in Antioch

There had been Jews in Antioch from the time of its foundation, mercenaries in the army of Seleucus. They were the original members of a Jewish community about which we are informed by the biblical books of Maccabees as well as the writings of Philo and Josephus and later rabbinical material. They prospered under the Seleucids, though they could hardly have remained immune from hardship under Antiochus IV (175–163 B.C.E.) at the time of his persecution of the Jews in Palestine. By the middle of the second century B.C.E. they were established as a *politeuma* in charge of their own affairs and situated in the southwestern section of the city. They were the largest Jewish community in Syria; some scholars place their numbers as high as forty-five thousand, others at half that figure.

They were governed by a chief officer or "ruler," acting, it seems, with a council of elders, representatives of the various synagogues. There are accounts of regular visits of Jewish high priests to the provincial capital, indeed one of them, Onias III, had lived for several years in exile in Antioch, where he was murdered in 172 B.C.E. According to Josephus the Jews of Antioch attracted much interest from the pagans in the city.

Our only firsthand information about the new community in Antioch comes from Paul (Gal 2:11-14). On the basis of the autobiographical details he provides the foundation of the community can be placed in the mid-thirties, perhaps as early as 35 C.E. Though Paul writes about a situation of conflict that arose shortly after the community's origins, he does not tell the story of its beginnings. Hence we are left with the brief note in Luke's later narrative (Acts 11:19-26). He locates the original missioners as part of the group scattered by the persecution after the death of Stephen–Hellenists like him and "men of Cyprus and Cyrene" who traveled north along the Phoenician coast to the island of Cyprus and to Antioch.

According to Luke it was the Jerusalem church that sent Barnabas to Antioch. A native of Cyprus himself, probably bilingual in Greek and Aramaic, with impeccable Jewish credentials and a well-established reputation for generosity in the Jerusalem community (Acts 4:36-37), he was the ideal bridge between the two worlds, a person trusted by both Aramaic-speaking Jerusalem dwellers and the Hellenist "men of Cyprus and Cyrene." To him, too, Luke ascribes the initiative that led to Paul's recruitment (Acts 11:25). Though some scholars contest the historical accuracy of these details of Luke's account, there is good reason to trust them, as also the information that Paul and Barnabas spent a year together in Antioch before embarking on their first missionary journey. Luke also includes a list of "prophets and teachers" (Acts 13:1), which adds three more names to the group of early leaders in Antioch–Lucius, a Jew from the North African city of Cyrene; Simeon, who was possibly a black African; and Manaen, childhood companion of Herod Antipas, the son of Herod the Great, perhaps one of his courtiers.

From Synagogue to Agora

In the persons of the first Christian messengers as they walked down the marble thoroughfare of Antioch on the way to the Jewish synagogue the gospel was making its transition to a new world. They might well have contrasted the world from which they had been expelled to the world in which they had arrived. They had left behind the Galilee of Jesus' origins and the Jerusalem of his death and resurrection. From that world of heroic monotheism and its group of competing Jewish sects they had come to a world contested by a whole pantheon of gods and many competing religions and philosophies. In contrast to the Temple in Jerusalem there was a bewildering array of shrines, sanctuaries, and sacred places that met their gaze in Antioch.

In the hospitable environment of the synagogue they were at home with an audience of fellow Jews, most of whom had lived the whole of their lives in this Hellenistic city. Their mother tongue was Greek; the Scriptures they studied and the worship they shared were in Greek. Though they looked to Jerusalem as the center of their faith, they shared with pagans in the civic and commercial life of Antioch. These Jews had a long experience of relations with pagans; even if they were no strangers to persecution or mob violence they felt no sense of inferiority or subjection. They had learned to live with pagans in a city whose official religion was polytheist and to explain and defend their faith in one God to them. In the process they had gained new members and attracted other god-fearers to their worship.

To this Jewish audience the visitors from Jerusalem brought a message that, for all its novelty, was thoroughly Jewish. Within the familiar framework of synagogue worship they proclaimed that the God of Abraham, Isaac, and Jacob had raised a fellow Jew, Jesus of Nazareth, from the dead. They argued from the Scriptures that God had finally fulfilled all the promises to the chosen people by sending Jesus of Nazareth as Messiah. To many Jews in Antioch they sounded, as they had to other Jews in Jerusalem, like publicists for a new Jewish sect. A number of Jews were convinced. From this audience, perhaps especially from proselytes and the god-fearers, they had much to learn about the way of missionary tactics. From the experience of these Diaspora Jews they could learn ways in which to approach the pagans, traditional Jewish arguments for monotheism, responses to the usual arguments and objections of pagan audiences, and quotations and examples from pagan poets and philosophers to illustrate their message.

When they stepped out of the synagogue into the agora, they moved from a center of Jewish faith into the heart of the pagan world. How that world looked to a Jew is well illustrated in the account of Paul's journeys in the Acts of the Apostles. To a Jew, the agora with its altars to all kinds of gods could well seem "full of idols" (Acts 17:16, 23). There the Hellenist missioners rubbed shoulders with magicians (Acts 8:9-12; 19:19), diviners (Acts 16:16-18), itinerant Jewish exorcists (Acts 19:13), and priests of the official religion (Acts 14:13). They encountered street preachers and philosophers of different schools, Stoics and Epicureans (Acts 17:18), Cynics in their rough cloaks with long unkempt hair and beard, staff, and begging bowl. They brought on themselves the anger of magicians (Acts 13:8), diviners (Acts 16:19), and guilds, whose livelihoods were threatened by their message (Acts 19:25).

To this pagan audience they looked very much like one more group of street preachers competing for the minds and hearts of their hearers, attempting to persuade them to a new way of life. They were different from the priests, diviners, and prophets of the traditional religions attached to a local shrine. They could not be confused with magicians and astrologers, though they were endowed with unusual powers, capable of evoking enthusiastic response from their audience and at times of startling acts of healing, which might suggest that they be classed with the prodigious wonder-workers known as "divine men." They were all Jews, perhaps dissident Jews offering a strange variety of religion closely akin to Judaism, though certainly not as strict as others in their observance of the characteristic practices of Judaism. The most obvious category in which they could be placed was that of itinerant teachers or philosophers, though their message was quite different from that of any of the known Greek schools.

In Antioch the good news was clothed in Hellenistic garb and enriched by Greek concepts and images drawn from the life of the metropolis and the agora. Like every one of those competing voices they attempted to respond to the anxieties and desires of their contemporaries, their quest for "salvation." At the heart of their message stood the figure of Jesus. They tried to reassure the pagans that death was not the final state of humankind, that their aspiration toward a worldwide fellowship could be met in the new community, that communion with God could be attained through acceptance of their message. With marvelous brevity Luke summarizes all this as "preaching the Lord Jesus" (Acts 11:20).

10 "For the first time . . . Christians"

The New Community

Gradually people became aware of a new kind of community in Antioch. Everybody who lived in the city was familiar with its great variety of ethnic and religious groups. It was a simple matter to distinguish adherents of the different philosophical schools and members of guilds and clubs and associations for all sorts of purposes and to place worshipers in their position inside the spectrum of local and foreign cults. The appearance of one more Oriental religion was not in itself unusual, but this new group was without precedent in any Hellenistic city.

Its origins were Jewish and it included Jewish members, but it could not be simply identified with the Jewish community established around the Daphne gate because, though some of these belonged to it, others did not. The pagans were familiar enough with the characteristic way of life of the Jews. They knew about their dietary laws, their abhorrence of blood, of statues and images, their careful attention to the details of the Sabbath rest. They had observed these things and many other practices by which the Jews asserted and reinforced their consciousness of their special identity as a people set apart, though for all its separateness, the Jewish religion had no difficulty in admitting non-Jews either fully or partially into its fellowship.

The new group was quite different. It had Jewish members and included proselytes and god-fearers as well, but it also included Gentiles, that is, non-Jewish members. What was unprecedented in this religious fellowship was that it was based not on a common acceptance of Jewish belief or shared worship in the synagogue or observance of Jewish law but rather on their acceptance of a message centering on one particular Palestinian Jew, Jesus of Nazareth, whom the Jewish members accepted as Messiah, or, as he was entitled in Greek, the *Christos,* or anointed one. Not all Jews shared this belief, perhaps relatively few of them; in fact, the issue was one that divided the members of the synagogue sharply, but those who did showed a degree of kinship with non-Jewish members—even those who were neither proselytes nor adherents of the synagogue—that made a striking contrast with traditional Jewish separateness.

The New Name

How long it was before this community received its distinctive name is not known. The name "Christians" was obviously framed by outsiders to the group because it was based on a misunderstanding of the title *Christos* given to Jesus, which it took to be a proper name like that of Pompey or Augustus or Herod, whose followers were called Pompeians, Augustians, and Herodians. It must have been coined by pagans, for no Jew outside the community would have permitted any possible suggestion that Jesus was indeed the Messiah. Citizens of Antioch had a well-earned reputation for nicknames, even for their emperors, so it is just conceivable that the name originated as a satirical jibe at believers in Jesus as Messiah. What is more likely is that it was a slang term to indicate a group of followers of the God Christos, identified as members of a new mystery religion. There are no signs that the term was in common use outside Antioch. It occurs only three times in the New Testament, two of them in Acts (Acts 11:26; 26:28; 1 Pet 4:16) and appears in the pagan authors Tacitus, Suetonius, and Pliny only after 110 C.E.

"It was in Antioch that the disciples were first called Christians"

A little reflection suffices to suggest some of the complexity of the community situation Luke summarizes with such deceptive simplicity. His neat outline divides the community's origins into two successive phases–the initial preaching by Hellenist missioners among the Jews in the synagogue, then by "men of Cyprus and Cyrene" among pagans in the agora–and underlines the later roles of Barnabas and Paul. His vignette concludes with an established community whose distinctive "Christian" identity is publicly acknowledged by all and which differentiates them clearly from Jews and non-Christian pagans alike.

There is much we should like to know about the early days of the Antioch community and the process by which that identity finally emerged into clear consciousness. Were there any differences between the Hellenist missioners who "spoke the word to no one except Jews" and the "men of Cyprus and Cyrene" who pioneered the mission to the pagans? Was there first a solidly established group of Jews in the synagogues of Antioch believing in Jesus as Messiah before the Hellenist preachers turned to the pagans? What was the catalyst for that decision? Was it perhaps lack of success in the synagogue or hardening of attitude on the part of traditional Jews? Who took the first steps to bring Gentile believers together with Jews? How were the Jewish believers assured that it was indeed the same faith they shared with these Gentile Christians? How did observant Jews ever overcome their religious scruples and human repugnance to extend this fellowship not only to proselytes and god-fearers but to Gentiles and converts from paganism, to pray with them and share the same table?

To most of these questions the current state of our information and scholarly research provides fertile field for conjecture rather than firm ground for final conclusions. Profiting by half a century of hindsight Luke simply presents the first and last links in a chain, the initial preaching and the distinctive Christian community fully established and recognized; the end result he simply ascribes to the mysterious activity of the Spirit. It is only when we turn to other episodes in the Acts of the Apostles and the epistles of Paul that we move beyond that simple summary to the much more confused details of the human interactions within which that distinctive identity was gradually crystallizing.

The process was neither instantaneous nor invariably serene. In these other pages we see bold missionary initiatives undertaken by individuals and groups creating completely new situations that give rise to unheard-of questions. We hear the first tentative answers of the innovators, their rejection by more traditional Jewish believers, the round of argument and debate leading to authoritative decision. We sympathize with the frustration of missioners whose successful efforts were being jeopardized by interference from opponents. We begin to appreciate the sensitivity that was needed in the early, awkward, ecumenical encounters between observant Jews and recent converts from the immorality and idolatry of paganism. We observe a leadership confronted by startling and successful missionary initiatives, under pressure from both innovators and traditionalists, called on for decisions that were as fundamental and momentous as the recognition of the distinctive identity of the community on the one hand, and as temporary and culturally conditioned as how to regulate intra-community relationships on the other.

From Antioch to Jerusalem and Back

The epistle to the Galatians was written by Paul in the mid-50s with what was obviously a vivid recollection of events that took place in the first fifteen years of the history of the Antioch community. In his angry words we can read some of the internal tensions involved in that early association of Jews and non-Jews, and we can see quite plainly the different attitudes within the community on its two major issues—the necessity of circumcision for entry into the community and the conditions necessary for Jews and non-Jews to share a common life, particularly to share a meal together.

To the Galatians an embattled Paul vindicates the divine origin of his message and his authenticity as an apostle. His gospel has proclaimed that access to God is available to everybody through faith in Christ, so that his Gentile converts are free from the necessity for circumcision and the observance of Jewish laws and feast days. Opponents of Paul, Jewish Christians, have followed in his steps and contradicted his teaching by insisting that the only way to enter the Christian community is by way of the Jewish faith, that nobody can be dispensed from the obligation of circumcision and the observance of the Mosaic Law.

It is not the first time Paul has been obliged to fight this battle. To his Galatian converts he rehearses the history of his dealings with Peter and the leaders of the Jerusalem church in the decade after 40 C.E. From him we hear the only eyewitness account of the Council of Jerusalem in about 50 C.E. Fresh from the success of the early missionary ventures to the pagans in Asia Minor, Paul set out for Jerusalem with a delegation from Antioch that included his companion, Barnabas, and an uncircumcised Gentile Christian named Titus. They met with Peter, James, and John, leaders of the Jerusalem community, who approved of Paul's message of salvation by faith and his missionary tactics of admission of non-Jews to the community without any obligation of becoming a Jew (Gal 2:1-10). Apart from the three "columns" of the Jerusalem community, Paul mentions another group in Jerusalem whom he bluntly labels as "false brothers, secretly brought in to spy on our freedom." These were Jewish Christians who disagreed with the decision of their leaders and insisted on the necessity for pagans to become Jews before admission to the Christian community.

Luke tells the story of the same meeting in different fashion (Acts 15:1-19). He places its origin in a disturbance caused in Antioch by "certain individuals come down from Judea" who insist on the necessity for pagans to be circumcised and keep the Law of Moses. In the course of the meeting in Jerusalem others "who belonged to the sect of the Pharisees" repeat this refrain. Within the Jewish Christian community in Jerusalem, then, even fifteen years after the origins of the Antioch community, there were still Jewish Christians who disagreed on this fundamental issue of the identity of the community, insisting that it remain Jewish. In the beginning there had not been the slightest reason to question that Jewishness; twenty years later, confronted with the radical views and practices of the Gentile mission, what had been an implicit assumption of their Jewish identity hardened into an explicit assertion. Despite the authoritative decision of Peter, James, and John in Paul's favor in Jerusalem, Jewish Christian missioners were still trying to impose their opposite view on Gentile converts made by Paul in Galatia the best part of a decade later. So far was authoritative apostolic decision from achieving immediate and universal obedience.

The decision to admit Gentiles to the community without first obliging them to become Jews was to have universal repercussions that have shaped its history to this day, but it created another situation in Christian communities that led to similar differences of opinion and eventually called for further local directives. The problem did not arise in communities, as in Galatia, that were composed exclusively of Gentile Christians or in those, as in Jerusalem, that were composed of exclusively Jewish Christians, but only in those composed of both Gentile and Jewish Christians. It was a matter of doing justice to the sensitivities of the Jewish Christians in regard to ritual purity. How could observant Jewish members possibly mix with Gentiles without doing violence to deep-seated Jewish feelings and even breaking the commandments of the Mosaic Law governing ritual purity? If they were to share a meal then surely the Gentiles should respect their repugnance for some foods and their fear of contamination by meat sacrificed to idols. Should not some minimum demands be made on the Gentile members for the sake of fellowship?

It is clear that the question was answered differently in different places. In some places where Christian communities embraced Jewish believers and Gentile converts the latter were obliged to observe the regulations of the Jewish Law governing the behavior of the foreigner resident in Israel (Lev 17:8-12; 18:16f.). These regulations appear in the letter Luke ascribes to the apostles and elders in Jerusalem to be sent to Gentile Christians in Antioch, Syria, and Cilicia (Acts 15:22-29), though they correspond to a different situation to the one that caused the Jerusalem meeting.

Antioch was the place where the issue came to a head in the celebrated encounter of Paul and Peter (Gal 2:11-14). We only have Paul's version of this episode, and it centers on a vigorous argument in which he found himself at odds not only with Peter but with his own long-standing colleague Barnabas. The argument was crucial in Paul's eyes; he staked his position in the community on it, and (though the epistle gives no hint of the outcome) this time he lost.

The episode took place after the Jerusalem Council (Gal 2:11-14). Peter visited Antioch and shared meals with the Gentile Christians there until the arrival of a group of Jewish Christians from Jerusalem, "certain people from James," as Paul calls them, to whom this kind of table fellowship must have looked like sacrilege. At this point Peter stopped mixing freely with the Gentile Christians. Other Jewish Christians from Antioch, who included Barnabas, followed Peter. To Paul this was "hypocrisy," "not acting consistently with the truth of the gospel," a refusal of the logical consequences of the decision reached in Jerusalem. To Peter, Barnabas, and other Jewish Christians, all of whom agreed in principle on both issues, namely that Gentiles could be admitted to the community without first becoming Jews and that Jewish Christians were free to share completely in table fellowship with Gentile Christians, it must have seemed a simple matter of prudence, a reasonable compromise to avoid unnecessary friction between groups of Christians of different views.

Different Groups of Christians

It is possible, then, to distinguish at least four different groups of Christians in the first two decades of Christianity on the basis of their attitude to the demands of the Mosaic Law. A first group, represented by Paul's adversaries in Jerusalem and Galatia, consisted of ultraconservative Jewish Christians and their converts, who insisted on the full observance of the Mosaic Law, including circumcision. A second group of Jewish Christians, such as James and the Jewish Christian community in Jerusalem that he led, did not insist on circumcision for Gentile members of the community, but did require them to keep some Jewish observances, particularly some Jewish dietary laws. The third group, best represented by Paul, consisted of those Jewish Christians and their Gentile converts who neither insisted on circumcision nor required observance of the Jewish food laws. The fourth and most radical group consisted of those Christian missioners who not only did not insist on circumcision or any other elements of the Mosaic Law but also saw no abiding significance in Jewish cult and feasts. It is likely that this group contained representatives among the Hellenist missioners who first evangelized Antioch.

Together with the diversity of attitude to the Temple, of which we have spoken previously, this range of approaches to the Mosaic Law made for a diversity within earliest Christianity that paralleled that within Judaism itself. This spectrum of attitudes, which can be documented in Jerusalem and other places not much later than 50 C.E., suggests a similar diversity in the beginnings of the community in Antioch fifteen years before.

Among them were observant Jews, persuaded by the preaching of the Hellenist missioners and believers in Jesus the Messiah, who still remained thoroughly identified with other Jews in their synagogues who remained unconvinced. These Christian Jews rarely, if ever, moved beyond the boundaries of their Jewish world to make contact with Gentiles, whom previously they felt obliged to shun and now were being asked to accept as fellow believers. Other Jewish Christians were more venturesome, particularly those drawn from the ranks of proselytes and god-fearers. Proselytes worshiped in the synagogue but remained in contact with their pagan families and friends; god-fearers moved even more freely in the pagan world while still sharing in synagogue worship.

Gentile converts, until recently devotees of one or another of the religions practiced locally, were enthused by the promise held out by the Hellenist missioners of a new life and new energies. They found kindred spirits readily enough among proselytes and god-fearers, who understood them and their world but surely found it more difficult to recognize fellow believers in observant Jews who previously had shunned them and whom they had regarded as religious extremists or fanatics. Some Gentile converts were completely disinterested in what they regarded as the rigmarole of Jewish religion and avoided Jewish company, associating almost exclusively with other Gentile Christians, at ease at prayer and fellowship with people like the Hellenist missioners and other Gentile converts, Christians like themselves.

Jewish Christians in Antioch may have found it as difficult to distinguish some Gentile Christians from the pagans with whom they mixed freely in the agora as some Gentile Christians did in distinguishing traditionalist Jewish members from the non-Christian Jews with whom they mixed in their synagogues. Between those two extremes there were others, Jews and Gentiles, occupying a middle ground that permitted them to maintain human contact with careful Jewish conservatives on the one hand and enthusiastic Gentile innovators on the other. Far from imagining the first Christians in the Hellenist world as a completely homogeneous community in which immense cultural and religious differences were dissolved overnight by the power of the gospel to create a brand new religious identity, we should appreciate this unruly diversity of many small groups—so different in ethnic origin and theological complexion, meeting in homes and synagogues—to wonder at its missionary dynamism and to ponder the source of the unity that gave such diverse groups a common claim to the title "Christian."

11 The Message in Antioch

Proclaiming the Lord Jesus

Luke describes the activity of the missioners to the pagans in the agora of Antioch as "proclaiming the Lord Jesus" (Acts 11:20). It is the most condensed summary in the whole of his two volumes. That skeletal phrase is fleshed out with no further explanation; no examples of the way they went about that task in Antioch parallel Peter's missionary discourses to the Jews in Jerusalem or Caesarea. In the absence of speeches from the mouths of those Hellenist missioners we are obliged to reconstruct the way the gospel was preached to the pagans from whatever other clues the New Testament offers.

It is obvious that the approach to the pagans differed considerably from that to the Jews. Indeed, Luke's summary phrase itself hints at this, for whereas in Jerusalem he describes the missioners to the Jews as "proclaiming Jesus the Christ" (Acts 5:42), these missioners to the pagans in Antioch are "proclaiming Jesus the Lord." In Jerusalem, too, Jesus was proclaimed as Lord (e.g., Acts 2:36), yet the term "Lord" carried quite different overtones in the Hellenistic world, where, as Paul said, "there are many gods and many lords" (1 Cor 8:5). In Antioch the title "Lord" was in current use by pagans to designate the gods they worshiped such as Isis and Serapis, and the Roman emperor was acclaimed as "Lord" in the ritual of emperor worship.

The difference between the way the kerygma was proclaimed to the Jews and to the pagans can be illustrated by a comparison of two discourses that Luke attributes to Paul, the first of which is addressed to Jews in a synagogue in the Diaspora (Acts 13:16-41), the second to a group of educated Greek pagans on the Areopagus in Athens (Acts 17:22-31). Though neither can claim to be a summary by an eyewitness, they both constitute what Luke regarded as representative specimens of the two different approaches. In the synagogue discourse we recognize characteristic elements of the preaching to the Jews—the recitation of the history of God's dealings with Israel (Acts 13:17-22), the testimony of the prophets to the resurrection (Acts 13:32-35), the appeal to metanoia, and the promise of forgiveness of sins to those who believe (Acts 13:38-39). Though the discourse to the pagans reaches the same climax in the proclamation of the resurrection and call for metanoia in view of God's coming judgment (Acts 17:30-31), it lacks those other Jewish elements and leads its pagan audience to that climax by arguments of a completely different kind.

Developing a Missionary Strategy

For an audience as ignorant of Abraham, Isaac, Jacob, Saul, David, and the prophets as they were of Jesus it was necessary to connect the kerygma with their history and their world. It was pointless rehearsing the history of Israel to these pagans and equally pointless to hark back to promises made by foreign prophets to people of another race who claimed to be especially chosen by their God. What was called for was a larger view of human history in which their Hellenistic audience could find themselves and recognize a providential guidance in their own history, to show that their own deepest aspirations as members of the human race could be achieved by the acceptance of this message.

We have already mentioned the kind of precedents available to the missioners in the work of their Jewish predecessors, the works of Hellenistic Jewish writers of earlier centuries, to recommend the Jewish faith in one God to their pagan neighbors in the Hellenistic world. We have discussed the kinds of approaches adopted in Alexandria. Though no such materials have come down to us from Antioch, it is a reasonable assumption that similar kinds of approaches to the pagans had been employed there in attracting converts to Judaism, proselytes, and god-fearers attached to the synagogues who now responded to the kerygma.

The experience of Christian converts from the ranks of the proselytes and god-fearers was invaluable in the development of this missionary strategy. Here were people who had been pagans who could explain what it was that had first attracted them to the Jewish religion, what it was in the religious aspirations of the Hellenistic world that found fulfillment in the monotheism and strict moral code of Judaism, and why, after being converted to Judaism, they finally had come to accept the Christian message. God-fearers could explain how they had found in the Christian message all they were seeking in the Jewish religion without the constraints of those elements of the Mosaic Law they were unable or unwilling to undertake. Where proselytes had entered fully into the Jewish world, the god-fearers had retained a foot in each world, the Jewish religious world of the synagogue and the Hellenistic pagan culture of their families, friends, and associates. They were ideally situated to explain each of those worlds to the other and to suggest missionary tactics when finally the Hellenist missioners bypassed the synagogue altogether to appeal directly to the pagans.

Instead of Hebrew prophets the Hellenist missioners began to draw on Greek philosophers and poets, in whose familiar accents their pagan audience could hear articulated their own noblest ideals and highest aspirations. They found allies among the philosophers in their critique of the many gods of traditional religions. In due course their pagan converts could be instructed in the Greek Scriptures, as proselytes and god-fearers had been in the synagogue, but their first concern was to connect their message with the hopes and fears of their pagan audience—with the ideals of Hellenistic culture and the realities of existence in a Hellenistic city.

The Kerygma to the Pagans

Our search for clues to the shape of the earliest Christian preaching to the pagans commences with the letters of Paul. At first sight this does not seem a very helpful starting point, for all those letters were written to communities already established in the faith. Paul's epistles are not samples of the kerygma that had brought those communities into existence but exercises in further education in a faith already established–explanation of its implications and exhortation to appropriate moral behavior. Moreover, the earliest of Paul's letters was written at least fifteen years after the Hellenist missioners began their proclamation in the agora of Antioch and was addressed to Christians in a different place.

Closer scrutiny of those writings, however, can take us back beyond those later situations and open a window onto the Christian world before Paul. At times he refers explicitly to the tradition in existence even before his conversion. When he passes on "what I have received" (1 Cor 11:23; 15:3), he is transmitting the tradition in which he was catechized either in Antioch or Jerusalem or perhaps even Damascus. At other points in his letters scholars detect passages where language that is uncharacteristic of Paul and other stylistic indications betray an underlying profession of faith or creedal phrase or traditional source older than Paul that he has incorporated into his argument. In other passages Paul refers to the way he first proclaimed the message to a Gentile community (e.g., 1 Cor 15:1), and this Pauline kerygma was surely shaped by his own missionary experience in Antioch.

The earliest of Paul's letters is particularly valuable in our quest. The first epistle to the Thessalonians is a letter of moral exhortation in response to the special needs of a recently founded Gentile Christian community that assumes and builds on the basic beliefs to which the kerygma has called them. It is written a very short time, perhaps as little as three months, after the initial preaching it recalls. Scholars judge that in this earliest of his letters Paul remains very close to the pattern and even the language of the preaching of Hellenistic missioners of the time, as he addresses himself to the details of Christian life in another Hellenistic city comparable to Antioch.

Before and After Paul

Three passages in this letter have attracted special attention as bearing the imprint of pre-Pauline language. In the first Paul recalls how they "turned to God from idols to serve a living and true God, and to wait for his Son from heaven, whom he raised from the dead–Jesus, who rescues us from the wrath that is coming" (1 Thess 1:9-10). These verses have been described as an outline of a typical Pauline sermon calling pagans to abandon all other gods, to acknowledge the one God, and to undertake a radical reorientation of their lives in preparation for an impending final judgment from which they are to be delivered by Jesus, established as Savior by God, who raised him from the dead.

Two other passages recall the shape of the Christian message before Paul. Reassuring the Thessalonians about the fate of dead members of their community, Paul reminds them of their belief that "Jesus died and rose again" (1 Thess 4:14), citing an early creedal formula, which can be found elsewhere in expanded form (1 Cor 15:3-7) and which enshrines the heart of the good news. In a final word of reassurance Paul asserts the saving value of the death of Jesus when he repeats another very early Christian phrase "who died for us" (1 Thess 5:10).

Scholars have pursued this quest for the pre-Pauline form of the kerygma to the pagans in much more detail, but even this brief analysis justifies the following summary: There is one God, Jesus of Nazareth is God's Son, raised by God from death and thus constituted Savior of humankind in order to deliver it from God's impending judgment; hence the pagans must embrace this one God, abandon worship of all other gods, and undergo a complete change of lifestyle in the believing community.

Thirty years after Paul we find these elements and much of the same language utilized by Luke. Though he does not provide us with any specimen sermons from Hellenist missioners in Antioch, he does at least offer us a glimpse of how the apostle Paul went about that task in the response of Paul and Barnabas to the pagans at Lystra (Acts 14:15-17) and in Paul's speech in Athens (Acts 17:22-31). Despite its telegrammatic brevity the former serves as prelude to the latter, enunciating the themes that are to be more fully orchestrated there. Once again we hear the call to turn from the worship of lifeless idols to the service of the living God, the master of creation and Lord of history, who is revealed in divine providential care for the world.

Luke's vignette of Paul in Athens is one of the highlights of the book of Acts. The apostle of the Gentiles proclaims the good news to a sophisticated audience of Greek philosophers in the very heart of the Hellenistic world. He presents his message as the ultimate answer to the religious yearning of that world, typified in an altar in the agora "to an unknown god." This theme is elaborated with the help of arguments familiar to Stoics and Epicureans in his audience. He allies himself with both in their criticism of traditional religions, of gods who are confined within temples of human construction (v. 24), placated by sacrifices (v. 25), or imaged in silver or gold (v. 29). He accepts the Stoic view of the unity of humankind and the kinship of humans with God, and like Hellenistic Jews before him he profits from a stock quotation from the Stoic poet Aratus to show that it is in human beings that the real image of God is to be found (v. 28).

But he departs from all those philosophers in his presentation of the one God who transcends the cosmic process and who, far from remaining unknown, has been making himself known down the ages through his care for humankind and his guidance of the history of all peoples (v. 26). In the past, Paul claims, God has been patient with humans in their fruitless search for him, but those "times of ignorance" are now past and a new and final era has commenced, the era of God's final judgment. Through the resurrection of Jesus God has appointed the judge of all the world.

Luke has fashioned this discourse of Paul as a model for Christian preachers of his own time. It is not a summary from a source close to the events in Athens and was developed over decades, but in it we can surely find the approaches and themes used by the first Christian missioners to the pagans, which were adopted from Jewish apologists before them.

Metanoia

Wherever it was proclaimed and whatever the audience, the climax of the kerygma was the appeal to metanoia. Addressed to Jews in Antioch, this did not differ greatly from the appeal to Jews in Jerusalem, though preachers could not tax Jews in the Diaspora with complicity in the death of Jesus as they did in Jerusalem. Outside Jerusalem Jewish audiences were called to dissociate themselves from the judgment of the leaders of their people and to accept Jesus, risen from the dead, as Messiah. No more in Antioch than in Jerusalem did this acceptance involve conflict with their profession of belief in one God or abandonment of the religion they shared with other Jews. Addressed to pagans, though, the call to metanoia involved a radical departure from their previous religion and way of life.

Not that a call to conversion was something unknown to pagan audiences. All the philosophers competing with the Hellenist missioners for the same audience in the agora–Stoics, Epicureans, Cynics, and Pythagoreans–were attempting to convert them. None of those teachers saw their task as that of presenting a series of speculative truths for intellectual acceptance but as one of provoking them to dissatisfaction with their present state in order to lead them to a new way of looking at life and a new set of moral standards. The writings of pagan philosophers employ many of the terms that later became Christian cliches; for them, too, to be converted was to begin a new life, to waken from sleep and live soberly, to repent.

The language that came naturally to Christian missioners when they described the kind of conversion to which they were calling their fellow citizens was the traditional language of Hellenistic Judaism, a language forged in the fires of anti-pagan polemic. When Paul recalls the response to his preaching in Thessalonica, he talks of the way they "turned from idols to serve a living and true God" (1 Thess 1:9). The Greek word translated as "idol" simply meant "image," but in this context it was a sarcastic taunt designating the representations of pagan gods as inert, impotent non-gods. In Antioch as in every Hellenistic city such images abounded. The statue of Tiberius dominated the main thoroughfare of the city; statues of various gods multiplied in shrines and sanctuaries; coins bore the image of gods and emperors. For Christians as for Jews the honor paid to these lifeless representations was an injury to the one only God to whom alone it was due.

The Living and True God

Over against those lifeless images stood that one God, "living and true," forever active as the controlling influence in the world and its history, reliable and faithful, especially to the covenant promise to the chosen people. The philosophers might deride the superstition and excesses of popular religion, but they too were culpable, because all their wisdom had not led them to the knowledge of the true God. Epicureans were agnostics for whom nothing could be known of the gods. Though the Stoics taught an innate human capacity to know God, the being they recognized as God was very much identified with the world itself. Paul's discourse at Athens presents an indulgent view of this "ignorance"; another view regarded it as culpable disregard of the God who inspired everybody to search for him and who offered so many signs of himself in creation.

The first step in the conversion of the pagan to monotheism, then, was not the acceptance of an intellectual proposition about the nature of God, something similar to the mastery of a new mathematical equation. Acceptance of the kerygma led to a new kind of "knowing," not of so many truths but of a living, active, personal being. What followed was a radical reorientation of one's life, a step across a threshold into a new world seen through different eyes and entry into a new society built on totally different values. The process of conversion initiated by the kerygma demanded the abandonment not only of the religion of the past but of the social context that it shaped and that supported it, the loss of many friendships and possible family disruption.

The ongoing process involved, in fact, a thorough resocialization in a new community, without the support of which the intellectual, moral, and social dislocation entailed could hardly have been supportable. Paul's letters bear ample testimony to the warm bonds of kinship in those early communities that sustained them in this continuing process. In the short term, too, this was favored by the ardent expectation of imminent judgment, which was surely as keen in the beginnings in Antioch as it was in Thessalonica fifteen years later. The return of Jesus as final instrument of God's justice was a powerful motive for perseverance in their new life.

Living in a technological era, a culture that prides itself on its understanding and mastery of the forces of nature, the mechanisms of human society, and even of the individual psyche, it is difficult to feel one's way into the psychology of persons in pre-scientific times. To them it seemed that the world was peopled by strange superhuman forces controlling the separate spheres of human existence, engaged in constant battles with one another, usually capricious but always unpredictable and beyond human control. To come to know the one living and true God was to be freed from an intolerable burden of fear and anxiety about a remorseless and destructive fate. Human life and world history remained as unpredictable for the Christian convert as for the pagan, but the one supreme being in whose hands they rested had proven trustworthy–master even of death itself by raising Jesus from the dead.

Creeds and Christology

We have pointed to phrases and sentences in Paul's epistles in which he draws on elements of the tradition before him.

These underlying creedal statements show that the central points of the traditional faith of the Church had already been shaped into terse and striking expression before him. It is likely that some of those phrases were framed in the earliest years of the Jerusalem community, while others were shaped in the different environment of Antioch, originating perhaps in the profession of faith made by Jewish or Gentile Christians at their baptism.

Such an early creed is at the basis of Paul's remark "If you confess with your lips that Jesus is Lord and believe in your heart that God raised him from the dead, you will be saved" (Rom 10:9). The obvious parallelism between verbal confession and internal belief explains the meaning of the profession "Jesus is Lord," for the present position of Jesus as Lord is due to God's action in raising him from the dead. To proclaim that Jesus is Lord, then, is to say something first of all about God and the way God works in Jesus of Nazareth, now that he has died and been raised to new life.

Pagans in Antioch expressed the divine honor they paid to their many gods by the title *Kyrios,* or "Lord." Christians in Antioch, like the Jews, rejected that belief in many gods. Nonetheless, they applied the same title of divine honor to Jesus, a title reserved in the Greek Scriptures to God. At one and the same time they proclaimed one God and acclaimed Jesus as worthy of divine honor. In this they clearly saw no contradiction. A little later Paul was to say, "For us there is one God, the Father . . . and one Lord, Jesus Christ" (1 Cor 8:5-6), thereby distinguishing Jesus as Lord from God the Father.

For these early Christians, then, the title "Lord" did not identify Jesus with God. It did two things at the same time–it associated the risen Jesus as closely as possible with the God whose honor he shared, and it distinguished him from the God who raised his dead humanity to life. Because of the role to which God had appointed Jesus by raising him from the dead, that is, by God's gift, the risen Jesus is entitled to the honor due to God. This is a long way from the developed Christian creeds of the fourth and fifth centuries and even from expressions of the later pages of the New Testament, but it explains the constant association of the risen Jesus with God in Christian faith and worship.

12 The Antioch Community at Worship

Pagans at Prayer

When Jesus taught his disciples to pray he warned them that they were not to pray like the pagans who "think that they will be heard for their many words" (Matt 6:7). He was not the first to criticize those pagan excesses. For centuries Greek poets had made parodies of this kind of prayer the stuff of Greek comedy. Greek philosophers like the Stoics and Epicureans asserted categorically that prayer was futile, for, even granted that the gods existed, they were far removed from human concerns or interference in human affairs. Ordinary people had learned only too well the harsh lessons taught by life in the Hellenistic city and knew from bitter experience that happiness, and even life itself, was under the control of mysterious and powerful forces whose ways were completely unpredictable. They struggled to placate those unknown gods as best they could. Little wonder, then, that their prayers often degenerated into a desperate invocation of a long litany of gods in the hope of enlisting the support of the appropriate power by calling on the correct name.

The locus of pagan worship in the Hellenistic world was the sacred place, and its focus was cultic activity. It took place in a temple, sanctuary, or shrine and consisted of ritual acts of many kinds, purifications, processions, dances, dramatic performances, sacrifices, and sacred meals. Animal sacrifice was often followed by a public banquet in which the flesh of the sacrificial victims was consumed, hence many temples incorporated kitchens and dining rooms. These festivities were usually civic functions–traditional rites in honor of the gods of the city or the empire or religious rituals aimed at ensuring the continuing welfare of the state or city. In smaller sanctuaries various cultic associations gathered to share in the worship of the gods of their homeland or the patrons of their guild or association and ate a sacred meal as guests of the god to whom the sanctuary was dedicated.

In the home domestic piety observed a round of special days as religious occasions–birthdays, coming of age, marriages, deaths, anniversaries of the dead. The more homely gods of hearth and field were honored by offerings at household altars and by simple domestic rituals in which women sometimes acted as leader or priestess, but neither the traditional civic religion nor these more simple observances could satisfy the deeper hungers of the human heart. The individual was left to pursue alone the quest for meaning in life as well as to confront the mysteries of suffering, death, and the afterlife.

The mystery religions attempted to fill this void. In contrast to the public, civic nature of traditional religions, they claimed to offer salvation to the individual through the private rituals of a close-knit group. The individual was initiated into the community through a secret rite that included a period of preparation involving abstinence from meat and wine and ritual washings and that culminated in a ceremony held at night in the inner part of the temple. So well did these initiates respect the secrecy enjoined on them that little is known of this rite of initiation, though it has been described as an experience of darkness, death, and perhaps also rebirth. Their worship included the dramatic recitation of the myth of the god, which was usually a story of death and return to life, hymns they composed and sang in honor of the god, and a sacred meal eaten in the company of the god. This was a different kind of religion from the formal public worship of the gods of the city by a gathering of citizens; devotees of these cults claimed a personal relationship with a divine being that guaranteed salvation, deliverance from the caprices of fate, and even from death.

From Synagogue to House Church

In Jerusalem the locus of Jewish worship remained the Temple and its focus the cultic activity that took place there, but in the cities of the Diaspora the focus of Jewish worship was the Scriptures and its locus the synagogue. Many of the Jews in Antioch who had accepted Jesus as Messiah never moved far beyond the shadow of the synagogue, where they had heard the preaching of the missioners–except, perhaps, to visit the Temple in Jerusalem. In contrast, the vast majority of Gentiles who accepted Jesus as Lord had no reason to set foot inside a synagogue in their whole lifetime. There were other members of the synagogue, though, Jews, proselytes, and god-fearers, who took the initiative and mixed with convert pagans from the agora. It was when this mixed group assembled that they could be identified as a distinctive group, or "Christians."

In Antioch the locus of Christian life and worship was something quite different–the private home. Just as the extended family or household was the basic economic and political unit of that society, so too the house church was the basic cell of the Christian movement. In recent decades these house churches have attracted the attention of scholars, who have shown how important they were in the beginnings and spread of Christianity through the great urban centers of the Roman Empire. For the next century the house church was to be the center of Christian community relations and missionary activity.

On several occasions in his letters Paul refers to these gatherings in the homes of persons like Philemon in Colossae (Phlm 2), Nympha in Laodicaea (Col 4:15), and Aquila and Prisca in Rome (Rom 16:5) and Ephesus (1 Cor 16:19). We lack direct information about gatherings of Christians in Antioch, since neither Paul nor Luke write about them, but Paul's correspondence with the Corinthians gives us invaluable insights into several of these house churches. It is safe to assume that the origins of the house church are to be placed in Antioch and that the pattern of life and worship in the house churches of Corinth mirrors that of Antioch, the missionary center from which they were founded.

The "house," or family, consisted of the father, his wife and children, relatives, slaves, freedmen, hired workers, and sometimes tenants and farmers. Around this nucleus gathered a small community that included some outsiders, perhaps of a lower social or economic level such as dwellers in the nearby tenements. These groups were not very large. Considering the size of houses excavated in Corinth it is not likely they could accommodate a gathering of more than thirty people, perhaps forty at the most. In most large cities there were several house churches; occasionally all came together in a gathering of "the whole church" (1 Cor 14:23; Rom 16:23).

The English word "church" is a translation of the Greek word *ekklesia,* which referred, in ordinary civic usage, to the assembly of the free citizens of a self-governing city. It is the term used in the Greek translation of the Hebrew Scriptures to designate the assembly of the Israelites, especially in their desert wanderings. It was in Christian use before Paul and was probably first used in Antioch for the Christian house church. It is important to appreciate the original emphasis on the gathering itself, the people assembled, on "church" as event rather than institution, as something that happens when Christians gather in somebody's house rather than the house or building itself. In due course Paul would remind his Christians of the larger reality, or "church," which transcends local barriers and in which the local community shares in communion with communities in other places.

This family environment influenced many aspects of community life. Leadership in the community was the natural function of the head of the household, whose legal power was considerable, though the exercise of authority was familial rather than military or institutional, and the position of leader was sometimes held by a woman, perhaps a wealthy merchant like Lydia (Acts 16:14) or a wealthy woman who owned the house. This environment also explains the strong emphasis on family virtues in moral teaching, its insistence on the respective position of masters and slaves, husbands and wives, parents and children, and the range of involvement in community affairs possible to women. The very architecture of the large urban dwelling imposed its own limits on the shape of worship.

The Lord's Supper

The earliest descriptions of Christian gatherings in the Hellenistic world are to be found in the first epistle of Paul to the Corinthians, written in about 55. In a long section of his epistle concerning worship (1 Cor 10–14) Paul deals with participation in pagan worship and describes two kinds of Christian gatherings in Corinth. In one they met to share a meal, in the other to share prayer and instruction.

In the course of remarks about Christians sharing in meals in pagan temples (1 Cor 10:14-22) he makes an explicit comparison between what he calls "the table of the Lord" (1 Cor 10:21) and the sacrificial meals of both Jews and pagans, each of which involves a sharing or communion with the divine being worshiped and with one's fellow worshipers. The point of the comparison is to insist on the shared life both with Christ and with one another brought about by the meal Christians share. Then an indignant Paul upbraids them for the way "the Lord's Supper" is being conducted (1 Cor 11:17-34). Poorer members have been humiliated and left hungry while others have eaten and drunk only too well. It is likely that the more distinguished members have been entertained in the inner dining room with fine foods and wines while the poorer were accommodated in the outer courtyard with sparser fare when they arrived later at the end of a hard day's work.

The significance of this meal becomes clearer as Paul corrects the abuses that distort it. He first reminds them of the tradition he handed on to them a few years before when first he evangelized Corinth, a tradition received "from the Lord," that is, from the community whose life Paul had shared. The recitation of the words of institution that follows is an excerpt from an early Christian liturgy, most likely that of the church of Antioch. "The Lord Jesus, on the night he was betrayed, took bread, and when he had given thanks, he broke it and said 'This is my body, which is for you; do this in remembrance of me.' In the same way, after supper he took the cup, saying, 'This cup is the new covenant in my blood; do this, whenever you drink it, in remembrance of me.'" Paul adds his own explanation of this tradition: "Whenever you eat this bread and drink this cup you proclaim the Lord's death until he comes." The celebration itself, the sharing of this food and drink, is a living expression of the meaning of the self-giving of Jesus in his death. In this way Paul spells out the implications of the tradition he received in Antioch or perhaps even Jerusalem for his Hellenistic community twenty years later.

In Corinth, then, this sacred meal was closely connected with the Last Supper of Jesus. It was eaten as a "memorial" of the death of Jesus, present among them as the risen Lord. The eating and drinking of that bread and that wine in faith was a communion, an entering into the life of the risen Jesus and the blessings achieved by his death and resurrection as well as with those who shared in it. It was a lived sermon, a proclamation by the whole community of the meaning of his death in the time leading up to his return in glory.

We have to allow for Paul's personal contribution to this understanding of the sacred meal and the way his personal reflection has already enriched the tradition he received in Antioch. We can recognize his special personal concern in highlighting the relationship of this meal with the death of Jesus as much as his resurrection because he does the same when he speaks of baptism (e.g., Rom 6:3-6). We need to note, too, that by the year 55 in Corinth the Lord's Supper was already a separate celebration from the meal that preceded it, whereas fifteen years before in Antioch this was not so. Apart from these distinctive emphases of Paul we still have a precious insight into the earliest understanding of this sacred meal of Hellenistic Christians in Antioch when Paul first joined that community.

There are other questions to which our sources provide no clear answers, such as how frequent these celebrations were and when they were held. In response to the question of who presided over the gathering and the Lord's Supper we simply presume that it was the natural leader of the household unless a visiting apostle or prophet led this group in prayer. From what we know of the Hellenistic world we would assume that if a woman was head of the household she would lead this family worship. What is puzzling in Paul's instructions concerning the leadership of women in worship is the seeming contradiction between his assumption at one point that women will prophesy in church (1 Cor 11:5) and his categorical prohibition of women speaking in another (1 Cor 14:34). Though a number of solutions have been offered to this well-known difficulty, no one of them has thus far gained unanimous agreement.

The Community at Prayer

Another section of the epistle offers a picture of the community gathered for prayer (1 Cor 14:26-33). Paul's instructions are aimed at ensuring the required order in an assembly where community prayer was not confined to the activity of a few leaders but where everyone was expected to make an individual contribution, sometimes prepared but more often spontaneous. These gatherings, unlike the Lord's Supper, were not restricted to Christian members of the household but open to strangers as well. They involved a high level of individual creativity, a mixture of ecstatic utterance and more measured discourse, of song and probably musical accompaniment. Among these activities Paul lists "a hymn, a word of instruction, a revelation, a tongue or an interpretation" (v. 26), and he issues directives for the activity of "prophets" (vv. 29-33), about whom we shall speak in the next chapter.

Embedded in the writings of the New Testament are other precious relics of the prayer life of the early Hellenistic communities. Scholars have isolated blessing prayers (Rom 1:25) and doxologies (Rom 11:36), shouts of praise (1 Cor 16:22) and confessions of faith (Rom 10:9), as well as prayers of thanksgiving and intercession. Some clearly go back to the earliest days of the church of Antioch, phrases that retain the flavor of their Palestinian origins, Hebrew and Aramaic words, acclamations to the coming Lord like "Maranatha" (1 Cor 16:22), the cry "Amen" (1 Cor 14:16), the "Abba" that began the Lord's Prayer (Gal 4:6). Others show quite as clearly the development of Christian prayer forms in the Hellenistic world.

Christian Hymns

A characteristic and essential element of Christian worship in the Hellenistic world was a new kind of hymn. The practice of singing hymns not only to God but also to Jesus is probably as old as the early Jerusalem community. As we have seen, the first Jewish believers found ready-made expressions for their faith in the risen Jesus in traditional Hebrew hymns like the psalms. In Antioch this stream of Jewish religious poetry and song flowed into a culture with its own long history of poetic creativity that had produced hymns to the many gods worshiped, either publicly or in private, by cultic associations and the devotees of the mystery religions. Now the traditional Jewish stock of psalms and prayers and its treasury of symbolic images was enriched by Greek poetic forms, rhythms, melodies, and probably new kinds of musical instruments and accompaniment.

Later books of the New Testament such as the epistle to the Hebrews and the Apocalypse provide a rich anthology of these new compositions from the worship of Christians in the Hellenistic world. These poetic pieces can be isolated from the surrounding prose of the letters by their metric rhythms, poetic structure, and their rare and unusual language. Scholars have shown that it is possible to isolate fragments and even verses of these hymns in the epistles of Paul. Some of these were probably composed for the worship of Christians in Antioch as early as the first decade of the church there between 35 C.E. and 45 C.E. At times, it seems, Paul is deliberately reminding them of their own songs, adapting by a few deft strokes a familiar hymn to serve as basis for his argument or moral exhortation.

Probably the best-known example of such a hymn comes in the course of Paul's exhortation to the Philippians to selfless service of one another (Phil 2:5-11). The hymn can be divided into six separate strophes or verses, each of three smaller poetic units. The poet or songwriter may well be evoking the figures of Adam in his search to "be like God" (Gen 3:5) and of the Suffering Servant (Is 53:12) in order to build the parallel between the humiliation of Jesus (vv. 6-8) and his exaltation (vv. 9-11). He sings of Jesus emptying himself of all that goes with his divine status to accept abasement, even slave status, and death. Because of his obedience God reverses this descent from the heights of heaven to the depths of degradation in death on the cross and elevates Jesus to the divine world as Lord of all the realms of creation, entitled to the honor due to the God with whose power he has been endowed (v. 11; cf. Isa 45:23).

These hymns were sung to praise God for the work of salvation and to praise Jesus for his part in it. They are also vehicles of teaching; they tell the story of the death of Jesus and his resurrection in a kind of dramatic narrative whose poetic imagery evokes their saving value. In their earliest form these hymns simply presented both the contrast and the intrinsic connection between Jesus' death and resurrection. Gradually they developed into celebrations of Jesus in his role in creation as well as in his mission of incarnation and reconciliation, which led to the universal acknowledgment of his position as Lord of all the spheres of creation and ruler of every agency, heavenly, human, and demonic.

The community's evangelists told stories about Jesus that presented him as a healer curing with God's power, as a teacher imparting God's wisdom, as the final proclaimer of the gospel of God. Its poets and songwriters present the work of God in Jesus in symbolic images that evoke that mystery in even more profound ways. They show Jesus as the human embodiment of God's creative power, the manifestation of that wisdom of God that presided over the creation of the universe and directed the course of human history, and the incarnation of God's Word, through whom the world was made.

Baptism

In none of his descriptions of Christian gatherings does Paul describe the rite of initiation into the community, and though it is impossible to doubt the fundamental importance of baptism, the New Testament nowhere describes the ritual itself. It is clear that the ceremony to which Paul refers in different parts of his letters was a bath in water, a complete immersion (1 Cor 6:11), probably in a stream (Acts 16:13), in which one took off one's clothes, descended into the water, was immersed, came up out of the water, and put on one's clothes, perhaps special white garments. Paul himself elaborates on the symbolic value of each of those steps.

This very lean summary of the rite of Christian initiation in Antioch can be filled out a little from two passages in which Paul incorporates into his own argument elements from the baptismal ceremony in the Hellenistic churches. In a brief phrase that form critics recognize as a baptismal creed we hear the cry of the newly baptized Christian, "Jesus is Lord" (Rom 10:9). In another excerpt from a baptismal ritual, classified either as a similar creedal utterance or as an extract from a hymn used at baptism, "there is neither Jew nor Greek, there is neither slave nor free, there is neither male nor female" (Gal 3:28), we hear the proclamation of an end to all racial, social, and sexual distinctions. Baptism was seen as the profession of the risen Jesus as the only Lord and as the entrance into the community of the new age, a community in which the unity of the whole human race was restored.

A religious ritual so natural and spontaneous as purification by washing in water was widely employed by Jews and pagans alike. It is not surprising that it was adopted as the basic ritual of initiation into the Christian community, the symbolic act that brought together Jews and Gentiles in one community. But great symbols not only have power to create and express the profound unity of a very diverse community, they also create a spiritual and intellectual environment in which no one expression of reality reigns supreme but where different cultures and sensitivities can thrive. For a believing Jew the ritual of baptism evoked biblical images and promises of the purification by the one God of the chosen people (Isa 4:2-6; Ezek 36:24-28). A pagan previously initiated in the mysteries of the Lord, Serapis might well have seen that Christian initiation as the true answer to his quest for liberation from blind fate, the terrors of earthquake, pestilence, and slavery, through a personal relationship with the only authentic Lord, Jesus of Nazareth, conqueror of death in his own person.

The Focus of Christian Worship

The worship of this community distinguished them from all other religious groups in Antioch. In fact, to many people they would not have looked like a religious group at all. They lacked everything commonly associated with a religion; they had neither temples, shrines, statues of their gods, priests and sacrifices like the pagans, nor synagogues like the Jews. The ordinary home in which they met for worship was itself enough to set them apart from both Jews and pagans, who gathered for worship in a sacred place.

It was not its locus, however, that was most distinctive of their worship but its unique focus on the one God present in the person of the risen Jesus. With the pagans Christians shared the universal human symbols of water, bread, wine, and oil, rituals of initiation and sacred meals. With the Jews they shared the worship of the one God with whom they communed by listening to God's word in the Scriptures. What was unique in their worship was their concentration on Jesus of Nazareth, established by the one God as the one Lord of their community. It was into his company they were initiated, with him they communed at his table, and his lordship they celebrated in song.

In Antioch the proper character of Christian worship became clear. The community's distinctive identity found expression in a distinctive form of worship. No longer could it be regarded as another kind of Jewish worship, a lesser alternative to sacrificial worship, as if "the breaking of bread" was something that happened on the way home from the evening sacrifice in the Temple. Well before the destruction of Jerusalem was to bring about the ruin of the Temple, the Lord's Supper began to stand out in Antioch as the central act of Christian worship.

13 Prophets and Teachers in Antioch

Prophets and Teachers in the Hellenistic World

Persons who claimed to speak on behalf of a god or under divine inspiration were part and parcel of the social, commercial, and religious life of the Hellenistic world. They were known by many names, one of which was *prophetes,* meaning "spokesperson," or "announcer," from which the English word prophet is derived. Other names were seer, diviner, sibyl, and mantis. Their function was to declare the will of the gods and predict the future, services taken as naturally in that world as those of the weather forecaster in ours.

The professional diviner claimed to predict future events by interpreting dreams, omens, and unusual happenings, by observing the flight of birds and the condition of the entrails of a sacrificed animal. Some of them were employed by government departments or the army, others operated on a free-lance basis and could be consulted in the marketplace for a fee. At the shrines of the gods, however, especially those of Apollo, the god of prophecy, people could seek a divinely inspired response to their specific questions. These were answered by a temple functionary, either male or female, who would respond with an oracle, sometimes received in a trance or ecstasy or vision, and uttered in unintelligible speech that needed interpretation by a prophet.

For many people these prophets and diviners were more accessible than teachers. The literacy rate in the Roman Empire never exceeded 10 percent, and although by the first century C.E.

there were schools where boys and girls could go to school from the age of seven, it is not known what proportion of the free population may have benefited by a primary education. Teachers trained the children to read and write, and they memorized passages from classical Greek authors, but the purpose of this schooling was seen as moral education.

The only teachers most adults encountered were itinerant philosophers like the street-corner Cynics, countercultural questioners of conventional ways. Those who could afford a higher education attended lectures from teachers who belonged to one of the traditional schools of philosophy, some as old as the era of Plato in the fourth century B.C.E. However much they differed in their basic tenets, all these teachers–Platonists, Stoics, Epicureans, and Cynics–were all agreed that the major concern of philosophy was ethics, or as they would have said, the moral formation of the soul. Right living is a craft to be learned, and the learning process must involve practice as well as theory. A truly happy life is one in accordance with one's nature, but human error and social pressure conspire to mask our true nature. Hence self-discipline is as necessary as right reason to achieve this goal.

From Kerygma to Teaching

The Christian community in Antioch, too, had its prophets and teachers, who are listed by Luke (Acts 13:1). There was no less need for ongoing instruction in Antioch than in Jerusalem; in fact, the complexity of the different groups only made the need more urgent. However much the groups who made up the Jerusalem community differed in mother tongue or attitudes to Temple and Law they were all Jews, heirs to a history that had begun with Abraham and to the promises of the prophets that culminated in the resurrection of Jesus the Messiah. The community that eventually came to be recognized in Antioch as "Christians" was much more diverse. It included groups who were Jews and groups who were Gentiles but more often groups who included both Jews and Gentiles. The kerygma, which had summoned Jews to faith in Jerusalem and Antioch, had been couched in terms of their history and its promises, but the kerygma to the pagans had been presented in different terms. The faith these diverse groups held in common and that united them in one community was expressed in different ways from group to group.

The community's teachers had a twofold task. They had to help both Jewish believers and Gentile converts to a deeper understanding of their experience in the light of their new-found faith and to articulate the demands of metanoia in their Hellenistic urban environment. In Antioch it was not only what was happening in the transformation of individual Jews and Gentiles under the influence of the Spirit that called for explanation but the unprecedented coming together of Jews and Gentiles in a community of faith. Jewish believers, proselytes, and god-fearers had to cope with the unexpected fellowship of pagan converts who shared equally with the chosen people in the gifts of the Spirit. Gentile converts who had previously been devotees of local gods or initiates of the mystery religions had to learn about the God who had revealed himself in the history of the Jewish people and now offered salvation through a Jewish Saviour. Jews were to learn that the position of the risen Jesus had eclipsed the Law of Moses; Gentiles needed to be instructed in the moral implications of their faith as well as the origins of the new community in the history of the Jews.

New questions clamored for answers. They were forced on Christian teachers by the way of life of the new culture they had encountered and by the events of their ongoing history. Some were as mundane as appropriate hairstyles for men and women in worship and whether one could eat meat knowing it had been sacrificed to pagan gods, others concerned sexual morality and community relations, whether Christians should arbitrate their own affairs or take them to pagan judges. The most profound of these questions concerned the very nature of the Christian God and arose out of the success of the mission to the pagans. If God has raised up a new people, is this not infidelity to promises made to the Jews of old? Apart from these new questions the old question of the crucified Messiah recurred with equal insistence if in other terms: How can a man who proved such a signal failure in achieving happiness as to die as a crucified criminal possibly hold the secret of the good life?

While patterns of teaching already developed in Jerusalem could be used in teaching Jewish believers in the Diaspora, new approaches had to be developed for Gentile converts. Illustrations that came spontaneously to Jesus in rural Galilee, agricultural images from farm or vineyard or scenes of village life, gave way to new images from the legal, commercial, and sporting life of the Hellenistic metropolis. Symbolic figures that captivated Jewish imaginations for generations were strange and foreign intrusions into this world. The vision of the Son of Man no longer explained their hopes for final deliverance to Gentile Christians ignorant of Jewish apocalyptic or unmoved by its dream figures. Even the Jewish term "Messiah," translated into Greek as "Christos," when cut off from its Jewish roots lost its significance as the title that had summarized the hopes of Jews for centuries and was reduced to a proper name for Jesus.

If the Hellenistic world posed new questions to Christian teachers it also offered them new resources. The first of these was the Greek language itself, a more delicate instrument than Aramaic, flexible, less tied to black and white alternatives, and more expressive of nuance. Greek rhetoric provided teachers with refined techniques of argument and persuasion. New images served to illustrate the work of Jesus, who could be compared with mythical heroes or men like Apollonius of Tyana, who worked prodigious feats and brought about miraculous cures and whose striking wisdom merited the epithet "Son of God."

Not all the images, symbols, and titles that originated in the Jewish world became obsolete in the Hellenistic world; some of them acquired a new significance. When Christians acclaimed the risen Jesus as "Lord" and "Son of God" in Antioch, they used the same terms of him as pagans used to express the sovereign majesty of the Roman emperor. When they designated the Christian proclamation as "gospel," they described it in a language that had already acquired a mythical quality in emperor worship and paralleled it with proclamations of great events of the Roman Empire like births, enthronements, and glorious victories. When teachers described the return of Christ in judgment, the backdrop they painted may have reminded Jews of the coming of the Son of Man on the clouds or the coming of God on Sinai, but to people in the Hellenistic world it compared that event with the solemn visit of the king or emperor to a city of his realm.

Christian Teachers in Antioch

How much do we know about the way those teachers went about their task? Luke has left us a list of the group of five prophets and teachers in Antioch. We have no records of the teaching of Barnabas, Simeon, Lucius, and Manaen, but we do know a lot about Paul. Once again we fall back on the writings of Paul. What we know about Christian teaching in the earliest stages in Antioch is based on inferences from his writings, written at the earliest ten years later. Paul's letters are prompted by later situations, but it is possible to isolate elements in the letters that can reasonably be ascribed to his training and shared teaching in Antioch.

The teachers began with the Scriptures, continuing the process begun in Jerusalem. It was probably in this ongoing reflection on the Scriptures that Paul was helped to appreciate the value of the death of Jesus as a sacrifice that justifies and redeems humankind–the means by which the sins that alienate it from God are destroyed (Rom 3:25). How much instruction in the Scriptures was received by Gentile converts we have no way of knowing, but parts of Paul's letters to communities of predominantly Gentile origin assume some knowledge of the Scriptures on their part (e.g., 1 Cor 10:1-13). There was already a developing tradition expressed in preaching, prayers, and creedal formulas on which they could draw. The teaching of Jesus was soon circulating in the form of sayings and parables. Paul pays little attention to the events of Jesus' life. He draws on the sayings of Jesus only occasionally (e.g., 1 Cor 7:10-11), but he attributes equal authority to utterances of Christian prophets, which he regards as words of the risen Lord.

Christian teachers made no attempt to develop a totally new system of moral teaching in the Hellenistic world. They subscribed to many of the moral precepts of pagan philosophers like the Stoics, Cynics, and Epicureans, though the motivation they proposed derived from their conception of the kind of people they had become through the work of Christ. Paul was to profit by the teaching of popular Hellenist philosophers in his teaching on conscience (1 Cor 8:7, 10, 12) and his presentation of Christian life as the fulfilment of the Hellenistic ideal of freedom (Gal 5:1, 13). Other Christian teachers were to exploit the conventional "domestic code," or lists of duties for members of a household regulating relationships between husbands and wives, parents and children, masters and slaves (e.g., 1 Pet 2:13-3:12).

Paul the Teacher: 1 Thessalonians

The clearest picture of the Christian teacher at work in the Hellenistic world that we have is in the letters of Paul. He has mastered the techniques employed by Hellenistic writers to interest, instruct, comfort, and exhort their readers and has made of the conventional Greek letter a vehicle for the communication of the gospel. He draws on the terms and images of the Scriptures and the tradition already shaped by Christians in centers like Antioch, and his letters are suffused by the warmth of his feeling for the communities he founded. From the earliest of his letters we can follow him as he goes about the teacher's task of helping those recent converts make sense of their experience as a Christian community and spelling out the demands of metanoia in their world.

He harks back to their initial experience of conversion when they accepted his preaching and thanks God for their faith, which is already a byword in Macedonia and Achaia (1 Thess 1:8). He has already given them instructions but writes "to restore what is lacking in your faith" (1 Thess 3:10).

He deals with two aspects of their community situation, their continuing experience of persecution and their worries concerning the fate of Christians who have died before the coming of the Lord at the parousia.

The first visit of Paul and his companions to Thessalonica had ended in an outbreak of mob violence incited by members of the synagogue (Acts 17:5; 1 Thess 2:2). The letter refers to the suffering of the Thessalonians and talks of persecution that has happened to them. Earlier Paul had sent Timothy to them from Athens "to strengthen and encourage you for the sake of your faith so that no one should be shaken by these persecutions" (1 Thess 3:3). We have no other information than this letter about these persecutions. The reasons are not stated; they may have simply been the growing "otherness" of the community, their abandonment of local and traditional cults, or the dislocation of previous social and family relationships caused by their acceptance of the faith. Nor do we know whether they were officially organized or whether they involved outbreaks of violence or other forms of social oppression, only that the Thessalonians suffered at the hands of their compatriots, probably Gentiles.

Paul helps them to a new understanding of what is happening to them by providing them with a context in which to place these events (1 Thess 2:14-16). He assures them that their experience is all of a piece with that of the churches in Judaea, where Jewish believers suffered at the hands of their brothers, and even with that of Jesus himself. The chosen people had suffered "afflictions" like this in Egypt prior to their deliverance by God; the sufferings of the Thessalonians should be seen as the prelude to the final deliverance of God's people by Jesus in the parousia.

The dead whose fate at the coming of the Lord so disturbed them were probably members of their own community but may well extend to Christians they know who have died in other places. It is possible that they were victims of persecution, in which case their anxiety could well have been even more acute (1 Thess 4:13-18). Paul approaches this problem in a different way. He recalls the creed they profess, that "we believe that Jesus died and rose again." From this traditional creedal formula he draws the inference that "God will bring with him those who have died." His inference is justified by a "word of the Lord," which is not a remembered saying of Jesus but the utterance of a Christian prophet speaking in the name of the risen Lord. This places the resurrection of the dead Christians about whom they are so worried inside a typically apocalyptic scenario in which it can be seen as the first act of the final drama, the encounter of the living with the triumphant Lord. The conclusion is clear: those who are living at the parousia will have no advantage over the dead; all will join in the final triumph on equal terms.

Having helped them to this new understanding of their experience, Paul devotes the final two chapters to moral exhortation in which he spells out the demands of metanoia. This section has a number of elements typical of the rhetoric of Hellenistic moral philosophers. It deals with topics that were commonplace among pagan writers, such as living a quiet life, monogamy and sexual purity, and the special affection due to family members. The specific moral demands or rules that he emphasizes hardly differ from those accepted as decent behavior in the pagan world. But Paul's appeal is addressed to them "in the Lord Jesus" (1 Thess 4:1) in virtue of the life they share with Christ and one another. The ethic he spells out is not that of a philosophical school but a community of believers, and the family affection is directed not to their own flesh and blood but to fellow Christians, brothers and sisters in the family of faith. Their ideal is not the good life of Stoics, Cynics, or Epicureans but a life of holiness lived in faith, hope, and love.

The Work of the Prophets

We can find references to the work of Christian prophets in Antioch in the Acts, but we must turn to the letters of Paul for a fuller understanding of Christian prophecy in the communities of the Hellenistic world. Where Luke provides names of prophets and vignettes of prophets in action, Paul provides an extended discussion of prophecy that assigns it to its proper place among the gifts of the Spirit. Better still, he talks of his own experience as a prophet, and it is possible to find samples of prophetic utterances in his writings.

In two places Luke writes of visits of prophets from Jerusalem to Antioch. The first is a group of prophets including one named Agabus, who predicts a coming famine (Acts 11:27-30). Later, after the Council of Jerusalem two prophets from Jerusalem, Silas and Judas, are sent with a letter to the Antioch community. But Luke also provides us with a reliable list of prophets and teachers of the Antioch church, which includes, apart from Barnabas and Saul, Simeon, Lucius, and Manaen (Acts 13:1-3). We find them at worship–in prayer and fasting seeking God's will, which results in the first mission from Antioch to the pagans. Doubtless it is through the utterance of a prophet that Barnabas and Saul are designated for this task.

From the earliest of his letters we can see that Paul assumes that the Holy Spirit speaks through the community's prophets. This is all the more striking in that the community he addresses is of recent foundation and predominantly pagan in origin. He insists that the prophets be not discouraged, though he does not automatically accept that every one of their statements is a clear indication of God's present will. Quite the contrary, they must be tested against the accepted customs and norms of the community (1 Thess 5:19-22).

With the Corinthians Paul engages in a long discussion of the gifts of the Spirit (1 Cor 12-14). Over against their enthusiasm for the gift of tongues he asserts the superiority of prophecy. Prophecy is intelligible speech aimed at the benefit of the whole community; its effects are improvement, encouragement, and consolation. However personally uplifting the gift of tongues may be, it leaves others untouched and strangers bewildered, whereas confronted by the utterance of the prophet the unbeliever or outsider feels "analyzed and judged" with inmost thoughts laid bare (1 Cor 14:25).

Scholars have studied nearly one hundred possible examples of these prophetic utterances in the New Testament and attempted to classify them as they have the prophetic oracles of the Old Testament. They have classified them according to their literary form into such categories as oracles of assurance, salvation, or judgment, and oracles enjoining a particular type of action or behavior. While some of these Christian prophetic utterances are similar in language and literary form to their Old Testament counterparts, it is difficult to isolate forms of speech in the New Testament that are so characteristic of the prophet that they can be confidently distinguished from the words of teachers or preachers.

Paul claims to be not only a teacher but a prophet (1 Cor 14:6), hence the details of his autobiography are descriptions of the prophet's experience at first hand. When he describes his call by God on the road to Damascus, he refers to it as God's revelation of the Son to him and parallels it with the call of prophets like Isaiah and Jeremiah (Gal 1:15; cf. Isa 49:1; Jer 1:5). He speaks of visions and revelations he received from the Lord, of being caught up to heaven and hearing "unutterable things" (2 Cor 12:1-10), so that he can say quite simply that "it is Christ speaking in me" (2 Cor 13:3).

It is a prophetic revelation of this kind that Paul seems to be invoking at times in his letters, either uttered by himself or another Christian prophet. Some passages that scholars have proposed as examples are the divine assurance of healing or support he received from God in answer to his repeated prayer (2 Cor 12:9), a prophetic oracle about the final age (1 Cor 15:51), the "word of the Lord" concerning the parousia (1 Thess 4:15-17), and an oracle about the fate of Israel (Rom 11:25).

14 Community Organization in Antioch

Social Diversity

We have already seen the kind of diversity in the early Hellenistic churches like Antioch that arose from the Jewish and Gentile origins of their members and the different attitudes they adopted to the Law of Moses, the Temple in Jerusalem, and the mission to the Gentiles. Other important factors heightened this diversity that were neither ethnic nor religious but social. We must also consider the social backgrounds of the first urban Christians.

Just how much can we know about their social status? It must be admitted that the evidence is at best fragmentary and piecemeal. When we put these questions to our New Testament sources, we are looking for answers they were not written to offer. We fasten on snippets of biography or local color in the narrative of Acts or names mentioned in passing by Paul in his letters or simply listed in their postscripts. Often we are simply reading between the lines. Sociologists, too, warn us against making a too-simple comparison between social classes in that world and social classes in modern industrial society, where often income alone serves as the index of social status. They remind us of other factors that serve as indicators of social stratification in that world such as ethnic origin, civic recognition, public office and honors, citizenship, the liberty of the freedman, and the subjection of the slave.

Despite the limits of the evidence the New Testament itself provides, scholars in recent decades have insisted on the importance of the social study of the world of the New Testament for a proper understanding of its message. Sociologists and anthropologists have tried to apply models developed in the study of other cultures to that of the urban centers in the Roman Empire. Social historians have squeezed every drop of information from inscriptions of various kinds. They have forced a revision of the view commonly held not long ago—that the first urban Christians belonged almost completely to the ranks of the poor and dispossessed—and have shown the range of social levels of members of these Hellenistic communities.

There is an inkling of this diversity in the only direct evidence we have of the leaders in the church of Antioch and the list of its prophets and teachers (Acts 13:1). If we exclude the names of Barnabas and Paul as outsiders, then these include Manaen, a Jew who had been brought up with the tetrarch Herod Antipas, perhaps as a foster brother and surely a prominent civic figure. Simeon is a Jew who also bears a Roman name, Niger, "the black." He may have been an African, as was Lucius from Cyrene in North Africa, probably a Hellenistic Jew, possibly even one of those expelled from Jerusalem.

From Paul's letters it is possible to compile a catalogue of sixty-five names of persons who were helpers of his or members of communities he founded. Thirteen more can be added from Acts. Most of these names lack any indication of social standing; there are only thirty men and women about whom we have any information other than their name. Sometimes, however, reliable inferences can be drawn from the name itself, since some Latin names suggest the status of citizen or freedman or slave, and some Greek names may indicate descent from the original colonists or settlers in an area. Ampliatus (Rom 16:8), for example, is a common Latin slave name. The Greek names of Euodia and Syntyche (Phil 4:2f.) may place them among resident aliens in Philippi.

The list includes people of means. Philemon owned a large house in Colossae and a number of slaves (Philemon 16). The house of Gaius in Corinth was big enough to accommodate the several house churches of that city (1 Cor 1:14; Rom 16:23). Titius Justus, a god-fearer and probably a Roman citizen, offered hospitality to Paul in Corinth (Acts 18:7), and so did the Greek Jason in Thessalonica, who was also obliged to post bail for Paul (Acts 17:5-8). There were prosperous, independent artisans like Aquila and Prisca, who were joined by Paul in their leatherware trade and who cared for him in Corinth, as they cared for many others (Acts 18:2; Rom 16:3-5).

There were persons of prominence like Crispus, leader of the synagogue in Corinth (Acts 18:8; 1 Cor 1:14), and Erastus, the city treasurer (Rom 16:23). Paul recalls a group who were "members of the house of Caesar" (Phil 4:22), members of the imperial household, possibly in Ephesus though quite as likely in Rome. These were usually domestics or members of the civil service, slaves or upwardly mobile freedmen or slaves, but the best-known slave of Paul's acquaintance was Onesimus (Philemon 10). The regular exhortations addressed to slaves in his letters make it clear that there were many other slaves in these churches.

There were other married couples, like Philologus and Julia in Rome (Rom 16:15) and Andronicus and his wife Junia, whom Paul refers to not only as having been in prison with him but as "prominent among the apostles" (Rom 16:7). There were independent women like Euodia and Syntyche in Philippi, active participants in Paul's work (Phil 4:2f.), and Phoebe, leader in the community of Cenchreae (Rom 16:1-2). There were women who ran businesses and had independent wealth, who traveled with their own slaves and helpers, like Lydia, a god-fearer and dealer in purple fabric in whose home the first Christian community in Philippi was established (Acts 16:14ff.).

Though we are a long way from a profile of a typical congregation, these notes and cameos still give us an insight into a multi-layered section of urban society lacking only its highest and lowest strata. Absent are senators and aristocrats at the top of the social scale and peasants, agricultural slaves, hired day laborers, and the destitute at the bottom. There are Roman citizens, freedmen and their children and slaves, though in what proportions we do not know. There are some wealthy people acting as patrons of household groups, and these included independent women. There are skilled and unskilled manual laborers. Most typical, perhaps, are artisans and small traders who together with freedmen were probably the most upwardly mobile persons on the social ladder of that world.

Gifts and Ministries

We are much better informed about the way in which those house churches were organized than about the social status of their members. In three places in his letters Paul lists the gifts with which the Spirit endowed the churches he addressed and the various ministries or functions of its members.

One of these (1 Cor 12:8-10) is a list of nine gifts of the Spirit, which is closely paralleled by another list of eight corresponding community functions (1 Cor 12:28-30). These Paul ranks in order of importance, "first, apostles, second prophets, third teachers; then deeds of power, then gifts of healing, forms of assistance, forms of leadership, various kinds of tongues." A similar list names seven functions (Rom 12:6-8), and a later letter written by a disciple of Paul lists five such functions (Eph 4:11), most of which appeared in the earlier Pauline lists. If we add the other ministers he salutes in Philippi, the "bishops and deacons" (Phil 1:1), we have a fairly complete catalogue of functions in these local churches.

While the variation in these lists suggests that some functions were more prominent in one community than another, there are some roles common to all. The regular appearance of the trio "apostles, prophets, and teachers" suggests that these are stable, permanent functions. Other activities like healing, miraculous powers, and speaking in tongues are more spontaneous, episodic manifestations of the Spirit. Somewhere in between come various administrative and pastoral activities. We have spoken in earlier chapters of apostles, prophets, and teachers in the Jerusalem community and in the Hellenistic churches. Here we deal with the role of apostles and other leadership functions in Hellenistic churches.

Apostles

Who were the "apostles"? The Greek word *apostolos* was not religious in origin. In secular use it designated a messenger or envoy, a person endowed with all the authority of the one who sent him. Greek-speaking Christians in Antioch used the term naturally to designate persons commissioned for various tasks as delegates or messengers representing the community (cf. 2 Cor 8:23; Phil 2:25). Paul's letters show that it applied to a wide range of persons. He recognizes apostles before him–not only those of Jerusalem (Gal 1:17) but also Andronicus and Junia in Rome, converts from paganism and "notable among the apostles" (Rom 16:7). Though he is very jealous of his own claim to the title of apostle and puts himself on a par with Cephas, the Twelve, and "all the apostles" (1 Cor 15:7), he still gives the same title to his associates, people like Silvanus and Timothy (1 Thess 2:6). He even concedes the title to opponents of his in Corinth whom he ironically dubs "superapostles" because of their imposing presence, their rhetorical skill, and other charismatic gifts (2 Cor 11:5, 13).

It is important to emphasize that Paul was neither the only Christian missionary to Jews and Gentiles in the Diaspora nor the first. We should not overlook the fact that his missionary career commenced as envoy or "apostle" of the church of Antioch as junior partner to Barnabas (Acts 13:3). About many of those other missionaries we know nothing at all–the founders, for example, of the churches of Damascus, Alexandria, and Rome. About the missionaries who founded the church of Antioch we have only the briefest of notes that show them as independent charismatic figures commissioned neither by the apostles in Jerusalem nor by another church but acting solely on the basis of their personal inspiration by the Spirit (Acts 11:19). We know nothing of the missionary activity of Barnabas after he and Paul went their different ways (Acts 15:36-39), but we can assume that he continued a very active ministry assisted by a band of helpers like Paul.

Through Paul's letters we learn of other groups of missioners in Galatia and Corinth, some of whom possibly claimed to be "apostles" or representatives of James or the Jerusalem church. There were some who contradicted Paul's teaching about the freedom of the Gentiles from the observance of the Law of Moses and flatly denied the legitimacy of Paul's own claim to be an apostle (1 Cor 9:2). Paul in turn labels some of them "false apostles" (2 Cor 11:13) and invokes a solemn curse on those who preach a gospel that contradicts his own (Gal 1:8). Christian communities were faced with the difficulty of distinguishing authentic missioners or apostles from spurious ones; and other New Testament books show that this problem of choosing between opposing charismatic figures, each claiming to speak for God, was not confined to those areas evangelized by Paul.

When Paul justifies his own claim to be an apostle, he asserts that his apostolate comes direct from God (Gal 1:1). Even if his first steps were taken as envoy of the church of Antioch, his special commission comes not from a local church or the apostles in Jerusalem but from God, who "revealed his Son to me, so that I might proclaim him among the Gentiles" (Gal 1:15). He is a founder of churches who prides himself on always breaking new ground, never preaching where another apostle has been before him (Rom 15:20). He formulates his own paradoxical criterion of genuine apostleship, one verified in his own career–the true apostle is authenticated by a human weakness and is one in which the power of God is manifested (2 Cor 12:9), in imitation of the death and resurrection of Jesus (2 Cor 13:3f.).

How other apostles exercised authority in the churches they founded we simply do not know. Paul's own style of leadership was both charismatic and collaborative. His remarkable influence was due to great personal gifts exercised in a preaching validated by signs of God's power (1 Thess 1:5) and a continuing warmth and affection for converts, whom he regarded as children to whom he was both father (1 Thess 2:11) and mother (Gal 4:19). He maintained an ongoing personal presence by visits to the churches he had founded and by his letters. If his claim to authority derived ultimately from his commission by God his teaching and admonitions were founded on the tradition, something he had received from the community and was as binding on him as much as on others. His arguments were based on the authority of the Scriptures and occasionally on sayings of Jesus but also on the customary practice of Christian communities and the demands of propriety commonly accepted in his society.

The pages of his letters are liberally sprinkled with references to his fellow workers, people he calls brothers, sisters, companions, fellow servants, or soldiers. There are at least twenty of these associates or staff members that he names, men like Mark (Philemon 24), Silvanus and Timothy (1 Thess 1:1) and Titus (Gal 2:3f.), women such as Phoebe (Rom 16:1-2), Euodia and Syntyche (Phil 4:2-3), husband and wife teams like Aquila and Prisca (Rom 16:3). Some of these like Mark worked with Paul for a long period of time, while others like Epaphras (Philemon 23), Andronicus, and Junia (Rom 16:7) had been in prison with him. Closest to his heart was Timothy, his assistant for fifteen years, whom he sent as trouble shooter at difficult times in the history of the communities of Thessalonica, Corinth, and Philippi. Not all of the people with whom he worked for a time could be regarded as his subordinates; Silas, or Silvanus, owed his initial commission to the church in Jerusalem (Acts 15:22), Barnabas and Titus later undertook independent missions, as also did Apollos (1 Cor 16:12).

Local Leaders

These itinerant preachers and founders of churches may, like Paul, have claimed a special authority over the churches they founded, but they did not remain as permanent members. Local churches developed their own forms of leadership. The example of the church of Thessalonica shows how quickly this might happen. Paul spent a few months at most there before making his escape (Acts 17:1-10). When he wrote to them no more than a few months later he could appeal to them "to respect those who labor among you, and have charge of you in the Lord and admonish you" (1 Thess 5:12).

Nowhere are we offered a precise job description for these local leaders. Their role is described in Paul's lists in different ways such as "forms of assistance, forms of leadership" (1 Cor 12:28), or simply "service" (Rom 12:7). Leaders are called "sharers, patrons, almsgivers" (Rom 12:8). These people care for, lead, admonish; they provide material support and management to the community. On one occasion Paul greets groups called "bishops and deacons" (Phil 1:1). The Greek word *episkopos,* which is usually translated "bishop" is found nowhere else in Paul's writings. In secular usage it meant "overseer" and has sometimes been compared with the role of supervisor among the Essenes at Qumran. It seems to have been confined to Philippi, where the "bishops" form one group exercising a supervisory function, either in worship or administration, and the "deacons" fulfill a role of general service.

Though Luke writes of Paul and Barnabas appointing elders for churches they founded (Acts 14:23), there is no sign in Paul's letters that any of these local leaders were appointees of his and certainly no sign of his dismissing them, even when there were flagrant moral disorders in their communities. He confirms their authority and urges "submission" to them (1 Cor 16:15-16). People became leaders, it seems, in whatever ways the community recognized and accepted their gifts. The leadership of the house of Stephanas in Corinth was due to their being the first to accept the faith there (1 Cor 16:15f.). It was natural enough for the patron who provided the meeting place, a person of means and generosity who was already exercising administrative skills in the management of a household or a business, to undertake similar tasks on behalf of the house church.

Women shared in many of these leadership functions. We have seen that there were women in the Hellenistic world actively engaged in business affairs, leaders of households and patrons of guilds and associations including ones for worship. There were limits to the involvement of women in public affairs, however, since they could not represent the community in legal proceedings. Euodia and Syntyche share the rank of "fellow workers" of Paul (Phil 4:2-3) with Timothy, Philemon, and others.

Of particular interest is Phoebe, a Gentile Christian from Cenchreae, the eastern port of Corinth (Rom 16:1f.). Paul recommends her not only as a sister in the faith but as a "deacon of the church of Cenchreae," probably the leader of that church. He praises her as "a benefactor of many and of myself as well," the official public patron or benefactress of the group, presumably a woman of means and hostess of the house church. Phoebe is usually credited with being the bearer of Paul's letter to the Romans, a role that implied presenting it to the leaders of the house churches in Rome and discussing its practical implications for supporting Paul in his projected mission to Spain.

Antioch and Jerusalem

Neither the church of Antioch nor the churches founded by Paul owed their existence to the initiative of the church of Jerusalem. The former was born of the preaching of charismatic Hellenistic Jewish missioners and the latter to the outreach of the church of Antioch. Paul in particular insisted on the divine origin of his missionary approach as apostle to the Gentiles and its independence of the leaders in Jerusalem. What, then, was the relationship of the predominantly Gentile communities outside Palestine to the Jerusalem community and its leaders? Paul had taught his churches that no one of them stood alone. Each house church belonged to "the whole church," which embraced the other house churches in the locality, and a local church shared a life in common with others. Was there a special place in this worldwide communion for the community of its origins in Jerusalem?

The Jerusalem community had taken an active interest in the early missionary initiatives of the Hellenists, sending Peter and John as supervisors to Samaria (Acts 8:14). Even the missionary activity of Peter in Judea had not escaped its supervision—or its criticism (Acts 11:2). After the foundation of the church of Antioch it had dispatched Barnabas to observe this strange phenomenon, and later two more of its leaders, the prophets Judas and Silas, were sent as representatives (Acts 15:27), the latter of whom accompanied Paul on some of his missions. We are familiar with the story of the visit of Peter to Antioch; it is likely that Peter also visited and preached in Corinth. Jewish Christian missioners claiming authority from James or the Jerusalem community were active in Galatia, Corinth, and Philippi. By the time James became leader of the Jerusalem church he seems to have exercised authority over nearby communities in Palestine and perhaps over Jewish Christian communities as far away as Antioch, Syria, and Cilicia.

Jewish believers in these predominantly Gentile communities of the Diaspora nourished a natural feeling of affection and loyalty for Jerusalem as the heart of divine activity in the history of God's chosen people. They dreamed of Jerusalem as the center of God's final action, which would reestablish the unity of the twelve tribes and make of Jerusalem the center of the great pilgrimage of the Gentiles. Gentile converts felt no such natural ties with Jerusalem and prized the independence of their churches, yet they could not but respect the place where Jesus died and rose again, the birthplace of their faith in the first Christian community. Jerusalem had been home to the Twelve and the disciples who were the living link with the earthly life of Jesus as well as first witnesses of his resurrection.

It is hard to imagine the response of the Jerusalem community to the extraordinary success of the mission to the Gentiles. Luke tells the story of the series of shocks they receive as first Samaritans, then the Roman god-fearer Cornelius and his household, and finally, in a bewildering crescendo, the very pagans in the marketplace of Antioch accept the word of God. By the time Paul arrived in Jerusalem with Barnabas and Titus, the leaders in Jerusalem were confronted with a decision for which they could invoke little by way of precedent in the life of Jesus. On the one hand conservative Jewish Christians were insisting on what they saw as a nonnegotiable demand of the Jewish faith, the necessity of circumcision and observance of the Law for admission into the chosen people. On the other the missioners from Antioch were demanding recognition of the legitimacy of their missionary approach of admitting Gentiles to the community solely on the basis of their acceptance of the Christian message.

The decision reached at Jerusalem involved several elements. The approach of the church of Antioch was acknowledged as legitimate. Missionary responsibility was divided into two areas, Palestine and the Diaspora. This recognized the independence of the Gentile mission, though it did not exclude the authorities in Jerusalem from intervening in the affairs of the churches of the Diaspora. The Gentile churches were obliged to recognize the special position of the Jerusalem community by supporting it in its material needs. Paul saw in this demand an opportunity for a concrete expression of unity between the Jewish and Gentile sections of the church. By their generous contribution of their material goods the Gentile churches showed their recognition of the origin of the spiritual blessings that had come to them through the gospel they shared (Rom 15:27).

Suggested Reading

(Apart from the works of general reference already listed at the end of part 1, the following books deal at greater length with the issues raised in part 2.)

Achtemeier, P. J. *The Quest for Unity in the New Testament Church.* A Study in Paul and Acts. Philadelphia: Fortress Press, 1987.

Bartlett, D. L. *Ministry in the New Testament.* Minneapolis: Fortress Press, 1993.

Branick, V. *The House Church in the Writings of Paul.* Wilmington, Del.: Michael Glazier, 1989.

Brown, R. E. and J. P. Meier. *Antioch and Rome: New Testament Cradles of Catholic Christianity.* New York: Paulist Press, 1983.

Collins, R. F. *The Birth of the New Testament: The Origin and Development of the First Christian Generation.* New York: Crossroad, 1993.

Cwiekowski, F. J. *The Beginnings of the Church.* New York: Paulist Press, 1988.

Kodell, J. *The Eucharist in the New Testament.* Wilmington, Del.: Michael Glazier, 1988.

Meyer, B. F. *The Early Christians: Their World Mission and Self-Discovery.* Wilmington, Del.: Michael Glazier, 1986.

Murphy-O'Connor, J. *St. Paul's Corinth: Texts and Archaeology.* Wilmington, Del.: Michael Glazier, 1983.

O'Grady, J. F. *Disciples and Leaders: The Origins of Christian Ministry in the New Testament.* New York: Paulist Press, 1991.

Perkins, P. *Ministering in the Pauline Churches.* New York: Paulist Press, 1982.

Wehrli, E. S. *Gifted By Their Spirit: Leadership Roles in the New Testament.* Cleveland: Pilgrim Press, 1992.

Witherington, B. *Women in the Earliest Churches.* Cambridge University Press, 1988.

Conclusion: From Jerusalem to Antioch

The Gospel Enters a New World

The three hundred miles that separated Antioch from Jerusalem could be traveled in about ten days along good Roman roads in the security guaranteed by the Roman military presence. For seasoned travelers of the time this was probably not a very demanding journey, but these pages have shown how great a transition it involved. The distance between the two cities was more than matched by the distance between the two worlds they represented, between the culture of Palestinian Judaism and the culture of the Hellenistic world.

Luke saw Antioch as a major milestone on the road that was to carry the gospel from Jerusalem, the center of salvation, beyond Judea and Samaria to "the ends of the earth" (Acts 1:8). For him Antioch was an example of the great urban distance between Jerusalem and Rome and places like Philippi, Thessalonica, Corinth, and Ephesus. The church of Antioch was the prototype of all the Christian communities of the Hellenistic world; in Antioch the gospel shed the original Jewish cultural garb it inherited from Jesus and clothed itself in that of its Hellenistic hosts.

The Gospel

Prior to the Second Vatican Council there was a widespread misconception of divine revelation among Catholics that virtually reduced it to a kind of divine message beamed out to the human mind. The gospel was understood as a treasury of divine truths communicated verbally by Jesus that provided a correct understanding of God and the kind of behavior that leads to God. The way God communicates through the gospel was confined to the human intellect, thus neglecting its impact on all the other registers of the human being, and to the individual, thus disregarding the influence of the community in which the individual's life is lived. It also disregarded the impact of God's self-communication in the material elements of the universe with which humans make up one cosmos, but, more to our present purpose, it took no account of the *cultures* that shape human life and development in those communities.

St. Paul understood the gospel very differently. For Paul the gospel is "the power of God for the salvation of everyone who believes" (Rom 1:16). It is a divine energy at work to liberate people from every kind of oppression–individual, communitarian, or cultural–that holds the human person captive. The gospel is, first and foremost, a way God acts, something God *does,* something that *happens* to people, which they experience whenever they respond in faith to God's initiative and accept God as God indeed. That divine action touches not only minds but hearts and spreads to every corner of the human being, even its unconscious depths. It affects communities as well as individuals, it penetrates and transforms the attitudes and institutions of the cultures that support their community life.

Experience and Message

People who have experienced God's salvation cannot but communicate this gospel experience to others. Like all other human communication, this takes place in many ways. The most comprehensive form of personal communication occurs through what we often describe very simply as a person's whole way of life, the complex of attitudes to life and its ultimate values, to other persons, to the choice of career and friends, and so on. The gospel experience becomes the gospel message when it is articulated in the spoken word, though words are never sufficient in themselves to convey the depths of that experience.

The gospel, saving act of God and human response, appeared in its most clearly visible form in the life of Jesus. The life of Jesus was God in action, the greatest thing God ever did; in that human career God asserted himself as God as never before. At the same time, Jesus' response was a total human acceptance of God as God indeed. His experience of God he communicated to his disciples through his way of life, his approach to life and death, his choice of career as prophet, his association with outcasts.

The gospel communicated in this lived fashion became the gospel in verbal form when Jesus articulated his profound experience of God's action in the limited human words of his preaching and teaching. The purpose of this communication was to draw others into his experience so that what had happened to him would happen to them. God would in this way become "king" in their lives; they, too, would "enter the kingdom of God."

The climax of God's action in Jesus and in Jesus' experience of God came in his death and resurrection. The risen Jesus is the final revelation of the gospel, of God's power to liberate even from death. That definitive experience of God the risen Jesus communicated to the disciples in all the mysterious ways by which they were brought to believe that God had established Jesus, crucified, dead, and buried, as the one in whose being God had irrevocably established himself as God the Savior.

After the resurrection the disciples in their turn communicated their experience of God in their encounter with the risen Jesus through all the activities that made up the way of life of the community that formed around them. The gospel, the happening they had experienced, was communicated first of all in the details of the daily life of the community, its worship, its koinonia, the care of its members for one another, even in the style of their community organization. Finally, that gospel was articulated in words in the message of preachers and teachers, and the gospel cycle of salvation was completed as others were invited into their experience.

Gospel and Culture

We have already considered the encounter of the Jewish faith and culture with the culture of the Hellenistic world in the three centuries leading up to the time of Jesus and seen the different responses this elicited from the Jews of that era. Many elements of that culture were abhorrent to them, and they vigorously rejected its polytheism and its moral laxity. At the same time, the Jews gave tribute to that culture in many ways, utilizing its language and literary methods, for example, to translate the Hebrew Scriptures and defend the Jewish faith. By the time of Jesus Hellenism had made notable inroads into Jewish culture and had left its imprint at the center of Jewish life in the Jerusalem Jesus knew.

It was a similar process that took place in Antioch with the coming of the gospel in the persons and message of the first Hellenist missioners and the birth of the Christian community. The call of the gospel to turn from idols to the worship of the living God was certainly a ringing condemnation of most forms of Hellenistic religion, but other elements of Hellenistic culture were gratefully accepted and pressed into the service of the gospel. The Greek language offered new possibilities for the presentation of the gospel message, and Christian teachers adopted Hellenistic teaching methods together with the best of the moral ideals of its teachers. Christian worship was embellished with new forms of prayer arising from a different sensibility. Christian poets and folk singers found new images to evoke the wonders of God's work in Christ, and Christian communities were organized in ways that arose naturally from the environment of the Hellenistic city.

The gospel can only be experienced and communicated in the forms of a particular human culture. There is no such thing as a "pure" gospel, untainted by incorporation into a human culture, because the gospel is not a system of divine truths existing somewhere outside this world and untouched by human feeling, language, and customs but God's self-involvement in the concrete circumstances of a people's history and culture. No one culture, of course, can do justice to all the riches of the gospel, not even the culture of Jesus and the first communities of believers in Palestine. In Antioch the gospel sought and found a new home and a new expression in the cultural forms of the Hellenistic world. In the process the Church gained a new understanding of its own identity.

Discovering a New Identity

In Antioch Jewish believers in Jesus were confronted for the first time with the question of the identity of their community. The first believers in Jerusalem and Palestine never dreamed of themselves as anything but Jews, like Jesus and his disciples. The differences between themselves and other Jews were no more than those that separated other Jewish sects from one another. The situation in Antioch was entirely different, for here Jews accepted Gentiles as equals in a community distinct from the synagogue, a community, moreover, that was perpetuating itself through a successful mission to the pagans.

In the transition from Jerusalem to Antioch all the purely Jewish assumptions in which the gospel had previously been wrapped were gradually laid bare. Not only were the limits of Hellenistic culture revealed by the gospel, so, too, were those of the Jewish world. The Aramaic language of Jesus and the Jewish communities in Palestine no longer communicated the gospel. Cherished Jewish forms of prayer and worship no longer spoke to Gentile hearts. Institutions as sacred as the Temple, its priesthood, and sacrificial worship were replaced by other forms of worship, and the Lord's Supper became central. Even God's supreme gift, the Law given to Moses, appeared largely irrelevant. The response of the pagans in Antioch to the work of the missioners and the manifest gifts of the Spirit they had received forced the conclusion that these Jewish cultural and religious forms, however well they had served God's purpose for centuries, were not an essential or enduring element of God's continuing work of salvation.

Antioch marked the first stage in the Church's journey of self-discovery. There it became clear that the gospel could not be confined to its Jewish cultural form, nor could the Church be identified with Judaism. The identity of the Church, like that of Jesus, always remains mysterious. Like him it is an agent of the saving action of God, which it symbolizes and proclaims, a community called into being and constantly renewed by the gospel. Its secret can never be captured in a verbal formula, far less a single word, but the pagans in Antioch spoke like prophets when they coined the term "Christians," because central to that identity is an attitude to God revealed in Jesus and a commitment to the way of Jesus that transcends all cultural differences.

This distinct Christian identity was not discovered overnight but only through a painful and protracted process. For Jewish believers this was an unprecedented crisis of identity. Together with the discovery of the place of the risen Jesus in God's work went the erosion of some of Judaism's most sacred certainties. Securities that had seemed guaranteed by God's promises to the chosen people had to be abandoned for an uncertain future in an unknown community. The process took place in the midst of factional conflict with an ever-present possibility of schism, of the kind of earthquake that would create an unbridgeable chasm between a Jewish church and a Gentile church. Even when, after more than a decade of uncertainty, an authoritative decision was finally reached by Jewish leaders in Jerusalem recognizing Gentile converts as equal members of the community, their apostolic decree met with something less than universal acceptance.

Unity in Diversity

Diversity characterized the Church's very beginnings. Despite their common Galilean origins there was diversity enough in the temperament and talents of the original men and women disciples of Jesus to ensure that their recollections of his striking deeds and sayings would highlight different facets of his character. We have seen the range of diversity in the earliest Jewish believers in Jerusalem, diversity in their country of origin, in language, in theology and spirituality, in their feeling for the Temple and their attitude to the Law of Moses. The gospel was proclaimed from the beginning in different ways to different Jewish audiences; Hellenist and Hebrew groups worshiped separately and in different languages; the needs of different groups of believers in Jerusalem itself called for a diversification of ministries and organization.

This diversity was compounded in Antioch. In Jerusalem the first believers at least shared the common bond of the Jewish faith, but in Antioch as Gentiles were admitted to the community the number and variety of different groups increased. Apart from the Jewish believers concentrated in the synagogue there were groups of Gentile converts and still other groups composed of both Jews and Gentiles. There was variety in the prayer and worship of these different groups. Some were content with the traditional Jewish prayers Jesus had prayed; others, unfamiliar with Jewish prayer forms, developed new ones under the guidance of the Spirit. There was variety in missionary approaches. While some continued their effort to convince the Jews, others developed new approaches to the pagans. The small size of individual house churches and the different personalities of their leaders were other factors that increased the likelihood of separate factions developing that would be at odds with one another.

Where are we to locate the unifying factor in all that abundant and even bewildering diversity? Certainly not in agreed statements of belief, common codes of morality, uniform styles of worship, a basic organizational structure or style of leadership. What unified them all, Jews and Gentiles alike, was something much simpler and far more deep seated. It was a basic attitude toward one man, a Jew not long dead, Jesus of Nazareth. They claimed that they experienced him as a living presence in their midst, medium of God's saving action and of the Spirit manifest in the life and mission of their community.

It was this basic attitude which they sought to express in their different styles of worship; in articulate and inarticulate speech, prayer, and song; and which they expressed in symbolic phrases in their slogans or creeds. It was to help them grasp this divine action in their midst that their evangelists retold the events of the earthly life of Jesus and their teachers spelled out the relevance of words that had been addressed by Jesus to Jewish audiences in Galilee to their different situation in the Hellenistic world. It was the living voice of this risen Lord that they recognized in the utterances of their prophets, and it was only in virtue of this commission that apostles and leaders could claim any authority to guide them.

No human gifts of organization, administration, or diplomacy suffice to explain the inner unity of such diverse groups. The preservation of unity in the building up of the Church was the purpose of all the diverse ministries, but the dynamism that sustained it was that of the Spirit. The experience of the communities both in Jerusalem and in Antioch went to show that unity was never something to be taken for granted. That unity was not an initial divine endowment that could never be lost. Quite the contrary, the koinonia that was the gift of the Spirit could be fractured by human failures and fostered by care for the needs of other communities–practical demonstrations of the kind of unity the Spirit inspired. The task of ecumenism in the Church is as old as the first community in Jerusalem, but it was never more urgent than in the new situation in Antioch.

The Continuing Journey

The journey from Jerusalem to Antioch is symbolic of the journey of the Church down to our own place and time. What happened in Antioch is what happens wherever missioners carry the gospel into a new world. The church of Antioch is the prototype of every community struggling to embody the gospel in its own culture. In each of them the Church is engaged in its journey of discovery, or better, of rediscovery of the gospel, of its own identity and mission, and in fact, of its risen Lord.

The gospel arrives as a stranger in a new world wearing the clothing of another culture. It only gradually finds itself at home with the language, customs, and institutions of its host. The settling-in is never entirely comfortable. Some elements of the new culture it rejects instinctively; with others it remains uncomfortable; while others it greets spontaneously and embraces as its kin. To their hosts the missioners bring the offer of salvation, affirming their genuine human aspirations and recognizing the gospel values latent in their culture, while at the same time unmasking their demons and exorcising them. From them it receives a new appreciation of what it is to be human and new possibilities of human community and, sometimes, a reminder of gospel values the missioners have forgotten or even lost.

At each stage of this journey the Church learns much about the gospel, which brings it into being as a community and which it must proclaim. It quickly discovers how much of the baggage with which the missioners traveled is truly evangelical and durable and how much is changeable–disposable cultural clothing, attractive, necessary, and perhaps indispensable for life and health in one climate but quaint at best in another and at worst stifling and repellent. The whole wardrobe in which the gospel had been clothed, from language and worship to ministries and community institutions, comes under scrutiny in a new world. Gradually new fashions emerge.

There is much to learn from a new world. Mastering a new language opens up a new mentality, another way of envisioning human life. A different approach to truth itself challenges previous ways of understanding, of learning, of teaching. A different appreciation of beauty stirs imagination and sensibility to new forms of art and poetry, of song and dance. A different perception of literature opens up new and fruitful ways of understanding the Scriptures. A different sense of the human person, for the relation of person to person, to the earth, and to the cosmos gives rise to new forms of spirituality.

In each new culture the Church rediscovers its identity and mission. Time after time the characteristics of the gospel, God's saving action in this time and place, are distinguished from the features of a parent culture and re-embodied in the new. There comes the realization that "Christian" is not a synonym for Jew or Gentile or Roman or European but for a believer in the risen Jesus. Christian missioners are not cultural ambassadors but ambassadors for Christ, and the Church's mission is not to export a cultural system but to embody and proclaim the gospel in this time and place. After centuries of imprinting its culture on other worlds a European Church discovers the limits of its cultural horizons and apostolic imagination and begins to grapple with the implications of being a world Church. Local churches move with increasing confidence to engage the cultural realities of their own world, to employ the new possibilities of communicating the gospel it offers, to re-deploy their ministers in new patterns so as to serve better the world in which they live.

It is hardly surprising that the journey is not always tranquil, that sincere Christians disagree among themselves about what appear to them as fundamental issues and even question one another's orthodoxy, that questions posed by new cultures do not find immediate answers, that authoritative decisions do not command instantaneous assent. Luke and Paul were only too familiar with this kind of conflict and discord in Christian communities from their beginnings in Jerusalem. None of them had impeded the progress of the gospel; some of them had triggered new missionary initiatives. Luke wrote in the comfort of half a century of hindsight that helped him discern where the Spirit had been moving in what he could picture as a golden age; the persons involved in the events were usually obliged to live with their uncertainty.

What, finally, the Church discovers on its missionary journey is none other than its Lord. Just as the God the missioners proclaim is not absent but unknown, so too the risen Jesus is ever present even if unrecognized. He is already present in the new world to greet his heralds on their arrival. Because of the solidarity between Jesus and humankind established by God in raising him from the dead, it is the features of Jesus of Nazareth that they come to recognize in the different complexion and clothing of their hosts, however disfigured by the demons of their culture. The Church's commission to "go and make disciples of all nations" (Matt 28:19) is not an arbitrary divine command, a test of the Church's blind obedience to its Lord, but an explanation of its identity. It is an invitation to go out to meet him in all the worlds in which he is yet to be found.